SCOTT FORESMAN · ADDISON WESLEY
Mathematics

Math Diagnosis and Intervention System

Booklet K
Measurement and Geometry
in Grades 4–6

Overview of Math Diagnosis and Intervention System

The system can be used in a variety of situations:

- **During school** Use the system for intervention on prerequisite skills at the beginning of the year, the beginning of a chapter, or the beginning of a lesson. Use for intervention during the chapter when more is needed beyond the resources already provided for the lesson.

- **After-school, Saturday-school, summer-school (intersession) programs** Use the system for intervention offered in special programs. The booklets are also available as workbooks.

The system provides resources for:

- **Assessment** For each of Grades K–6, a Diagnostic Test is provided that assesses that grade. Use a test at the start of the year for entry-level assessment or anytime during the year as a summative evaluation.

- **Diagnosis** An item analysis identifies areas where intervention is needed.

- **Intervention** Booklets A–M identify specific topics and assign a number to each topic, for example, A12 or E10. For each topic, there is a page of Intervention Practice and a two-page Intervention Lesson that cover the same content taught in a lesson of the program.

- **Monitoring** The Teaching Guide provides both Individual Record Forms and Class Record Forms to monitor student progress.

Editorial Offices: Glenview, Illinois • Parsippany, New Jersey • New York, New York

Sales Offices: Needham, Massachusetts • Duluth, Georgia • Glenview, Illinois
Coppell, Texas • Ontario, California • Mesa, Arizona

ISBN: 0-328-07654-6

Copyright © Pearson Education, Inc.
All Rights Reserved. Printed in the United States of America. This publication or parts thereof, may be used with appropriate equipment to reproduce copies for classroom use only.

4 5 6 7 8 9 10 V084 12 11 10 09 08 07 06 05

Table of Contents

		Intervention Lesson Pages	Intervention Practice Pages	The same content is taught in the Scott Foresman-Addison Wesley Mathematics Program			
Booklet K				Gr. 3	Gr. 4	Gr. 5	Gr. 6
Measurement Units							
K1	Measuring Length to $\frac{1}{2}$ and $\frac{1}{4}$ Inch	1	115	9-12, 9-13	10-8		
K2	Using Customary Units of Length	3	116	9-14, 9-15	10-7	9-1	
K3	Measure to $\frac{1}{8}$ Inch	5	117			9-2	
K4	Customary Units of Measurement	7	118				10-1
K5	Using Metric Units of Length	9	119	10-6, 10-7	11-9	9-3	
K6	Using Customary Units of Capacity	11	120	12-1	10-9	10-6	
K7	Using Milliliters and Liters	13	121	12-2	11-10	10-7	
K8	Using Ounces and Pounds	15	122	12-4	10-10	10-8	
K9	Using Grams and Kilograms	17	123	12-5	11-11	10-9	
K10	Metric Units of Measurement	19	124			9-4	10-2
K11	Time to the Quarter-Hour	21	125	4-1			
K12	Telling Time	23	126	4-2			
K13	Telling Time	25	127	4-1			
K14	Units of Time	27	128		4-2	9-12	
K15	Elapsed Time	29	129	4-3			
K16	Elapsed Time; Schedules	31	130	4-3	9-13	10-5	
K17	Using a Calendar	33	131	4-4	4-5		
K18	Time Zones	35	132		4-5		
K19	Converting Units	37	133			10-11, 11-12	
K20	Temperature	39	134	12-6			
K21	Temperature	41	135		11-14	9-14	
K22	Units of Measure and Precision	43	136				10-3
K23	Converting Between Measurement Systems	45	137				10-4
Perimeter, Area, Volume, Surface Area							
K24	Perimeter	47	138	8-11			
K25	Area	49	139	8-12	8-11	9-7	
K26	Perimeter	51	140		8-10	9-5	10-7
K27	Circumference	53	141			9-6	10-11
K28	Area	55	142			9-8, 9-9	10-8
K29	Area	57	143			9-10	10-10
K30	Areas of Irregular Figures	59	144			9-10	
K31	Rectangles with the Same Area	61	145				10-9
K32	Area of a Circle	63	146				10-12
K33	Surface Area	65	147			10-3	10-15
K34	Comparing Volume and Surface Area	67	148			10-3	
K35	Volume	69	149	8-13	8-13		
K36	Volume	71	150			10-5	
K37	Volume of Triangular Prisms and Cylinders	73	151				10-16

iii

Table of Contents (continued)

		Intervention Lesson Pages	Intervention Practice Pages	\multicolumn{4}{l}{The same content is taught in the Scott Foresman-Addison Wesley Mathematics Program}			
				Gr. 3	Gr. 4	Gr. 5	Gr. 6
Booklet K							
Geometry							
K38	Solid Figures	75	152	8-1, 8-2	8-1		
K39	Lines, Segments, Rays, and Angles	77	153	8-4, 8-5			
K40	Plane Figures	79	154	8-6			
K41	Classifying Triangles Using Sides and Angles	81	155	8-7	8-4		
K42	Quadrilaterals	83	156	8-8	8-4		
K43	Slides, Flips, and Turns	85	157	8-9	8-6		
K44	Line Symmetry	87	158	8-10	8-7	6-11	9-13
K45	Polygons	89	159		8-2	6-4	9-6
K46	Geometric Ideas	91	160		8-3	6-1	9-1
K47	Circles	93	161		8-5	6-3	9-9
K48	Congruent and Similar Figures	95	162		8-6, 8-8	6-9	9-10
K49	Measuring and Classifying Angles	97	163			6-2	9-2
K50	Triangles	99	164			6-5	9-7
K51	Quadrilaterals	101	165			6-6	9-8
K52	Transformations	103	166			6-10	9-11
K53	Solid Figures	105	167			10-1	10-14
K54	Views of Solid Figures	107	168			10-2	
K55	Angle Pairs	109	169				9-3
K56	Constructions	111	170				9-4
K57	Tessellations	113	171				9-14

Name _____

Intervention Lesson **K1**

Math Diagnosis and Intervention System

Measuring Length to $\frac{1}{2}$ and $\frac{1}{4}$ Inch

Example 1

When measuring to the nearest inch, only look at marks that are a multiple of 1 inch, such as 1 inch, 2 inches, and 3 inches.

The nail is closest to the __1__ inch mark.

The crayon is closest to the __2__ inch mark.

Example 2

When measuring to the nearest $\frac{1}{2}$ inch, only look at the marks that are multiples of $\frac{1}{2}$ inch, such as 1, $1\frac{1}{2}$, 2, and $2\frac{1}{2}$ inches.

To the nearest $\frac{1}{2}$ inch, the nail is $1\frac{1}{2}$ inches and the crayon is 2 inches.

Example 3

The marks on this ruler are each $\frac{1}{4}$ inch apart. When measuring to the nearest $\frac{1}{4}$ inch, look at all of the marks. To the nearest $\frac{1}{4}$ inch, the nail is $1\frac{1}{4}$ inch long and the crayon is 2 inches long.

Measure to the nearest inch.

1. The crayon is
_____ long.

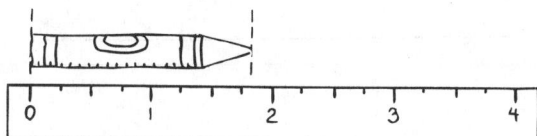

2. The caterpillar is
_____ long.

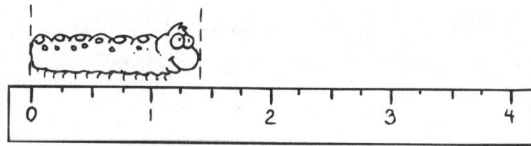

1

Name _____

Intervention Lesson **K1**

Measuring (continued)

Measure each item to the nearest $\frac{1}{2}$ inch and $\frac{1}{4}$ inch.

3. Nearest $\frac{1}{2}$ inch: ____ inches

   Nearest $\frac{1}{4}$ inch: ____ inches

   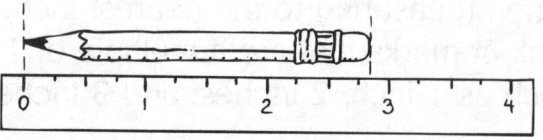

4. Nearest $\frac{1}{2}$ inch: ____ inches

   Nearest $\frac{1}{4}$ inch: ____ inches

   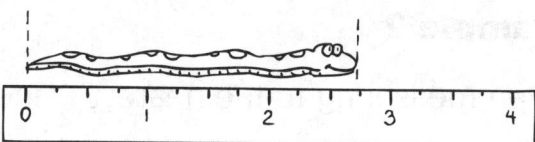

5. Nearest $\frac{1}{2}$ inch: ____ inches

   Nearest $\frac{1}{4}$ inch: ____ inches

   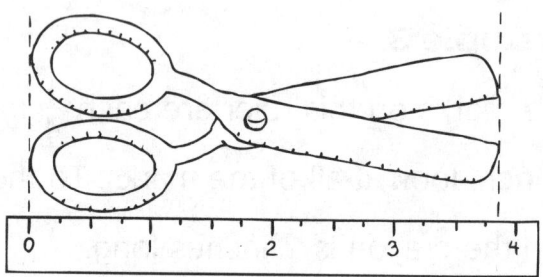

6. Nearest $\frac{1}{2}$ inch: ____ inches

   Nearest $\frac{1}{4}$ inch: ____ inches

   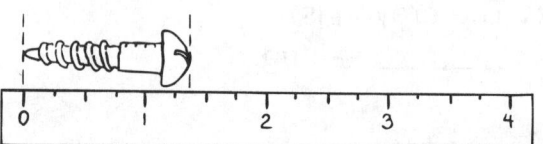

Name _____

Math Diagnosis and Intervention System
Intervention Lesson **K2**

Using Customary Units of Length

Example 1

Would you use *inches, feet, yards,* or *miles* to measure the length of a highway?

Think:
A highway is much longer than 1 inch, 1 foot, or 1 yard.

Since *miles* is the longest of the four units of measure, the length of the highway is best measured in miles.

Example 2

Find the missing number.

24 inches = ■ feet

Since there are 12 inches in a foot, and 12 inches + 12 inches = 24 inches, there are 2 feet in 24 inches.

Estimate each length.
Then measure to the nearest $\frac{1}{2}$ inch.

1. A clothespin

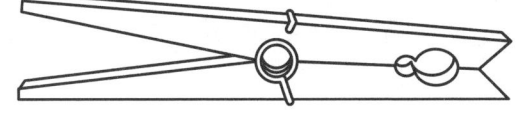

2. A key

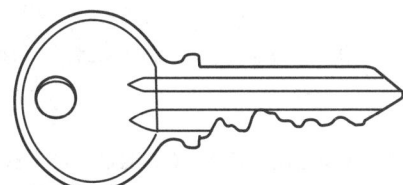

_____   _____

Find each missing number.

3. 1 yd = _____ ft   **4.** 3 ft = _____ in.   **5.** _____ in. = 1 yd

6. 5,280 ft = _____ mi **7.** _____ in. = 5 ft   **8.** 1,760 yd = _____ mi

9. 2 yd = _____ in.   **10.** _____ ft = 48 in.   **11.** _____ ft = 4 yd

3

Name _____

Math Diagnosis and Intervention System
Intervention Lesson **K2**

Using Customary Units of Length (continued)

Estimate each length.
Then measure to the nearest $\frac{1}{4}$ inch.

12. An earthworm

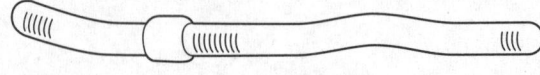

_____

13. An eraser

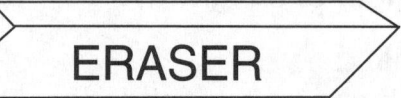

_____

Which unit would you use to measure each item? Write *inch*, *foot*, *yard*, or *mile*.

14. The length of a gerbil

_____

15. The length of a football field

_____

16. The height of a door

_____

17. The distance to the sun

_____

Find each missing number.

18. 2 yd = _____ ft   **19.** _____ ft = 6 yd   **20.** 2 ft = _____ in.

21. _____ ft = 72 in.   **22.** 108 in. = _____ yd   **23.** 4 yd = _____ in.

Test Prep Circle the correct letter for the answer.

24. What is the length of the cricket, measured to the nearest $\frac{1}{4}$ inch?

A 1 inch   **C** $1\frac{1}{2}$ inches

B $1\frac{1}{4}$ inches   **D** $1\frac{3}{4}$ inches

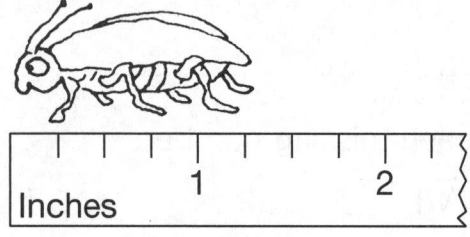

4

Measure to $\frac{1}{8}$ Inch

Intervention Lesson **K3**

Example

You can use a ruler to measure objects to the nearest inch, $\frac{1}{2}$ inch, $\frac{1}{4}$ inch or $\frac{1}{8}$ inch.

The pencil is between 2 and 3 inches long.

To the nearest inch, the pencil is 3 inches long.

To the nearest $\frac{1}{2}$ inch, the pencil is $2\frac{1}{2}$ inches long.

To the nearest $\frac{1}{4}$ inch, the pencil is $2\frac{3}{4}$ inches long.

To the nearest $\frac{1}{8}$ inch, the pencil is $2\frac{5}{8}$ inches long.

To measure to the nearest $\frac{1}{8}$ inch, follow these steps.

Step 1: Make sure that the zero mark (or end of the ruler) is lined up with one end of the object you are measuring.

Step 2: Find the $\frac{1}{8}$-inch mark that the other end of the object is closest to.

Measure each object to the nearest inch, $\frac{1}{2}$ inch, $\frac{1}{4}$ inch, and $\frac{1}{8}$ inch.

1.

nearest inch _____   nearest $\frac{1}{2}$ inch _____

nearest $\frac{1}{4}$ inch _____   nearest $\frac{1}{8}$ inch _____

2.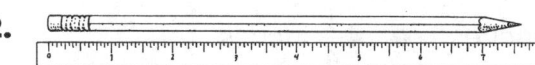

nearest inch _____   nearest $\frac{1}{2}$ inch _____

nearest $\frac{1}{4}$ inch _____   nearest $\frac{1}{8}$ inch _____

Name _____

Intervention Lesson **K3**

Math Diagnosis and Intervention System

Measure to $\frac{1}{8}$ Inch (continued)

Measure each line to the nearest inch, $\frac{1}{2}$ inch, $\frac{1}{4}$ inch, and $\frac{1}{8}$ inch.

3. ━━━━━━━━━━━━━━ 4. ━━━━━━

_____ _____

5. ━━━━━━━━━━━━━━━━━ 6. ━━━━━━━━━━━━━━━━━━━━━

_____ _____

7. ━━━━━━━━━━ 8. ━━━━━

_____ _____

Use your ruler to draw a line segment of each length.

9. $\frac{3}{8}$ in.   10. $3\frac{3}{4}$ in.   11. $2\frac{1}{4}$ in.

12. $4\frac{1}{2}$ in.   13. $1\frac{7}{8}$ in.   14. $5\frac{5}{8}$ in.

15. **Writing in Math** Which ruler will give you a more precise measurement: one marked with $\frac{1}{4}$-inch units or one marked with $\frac{1}{2}$-inch units?

_____

_____

Test Prep Circle the correct letter for the answer.

16. What is the length of the object shown?

━━━━━━━━━━━━━━━━━━━━━

A $2\frac{1}{4}$ inches   **B** $3\frac{7}{8}$ inches   **C** $3\frac{1}{2}$ inches   **D** $4\frac{1}{4}$ inches

Name _____

Intervention Lesson **K4**

Customary Units of Measurement

Example 1

For a party, 192 fluid ounces of fruit juice was put in 1-cup containers. How many cups is this?

To change from a smaller unit to a larger unit, divide.

192 fluid ounces = ■ cups

192 ÷ 8 = 24

192 fluid ounces = 24 cups

| 1 c = 8 fl oz |

Example 2

How many inches is 4 yards?

To change from a larger unit to a smaller unit, multiply.

4 yards = ■ inches

4 × 36 = 144

4 yards = 144 inches

| 1 yd = 36 in. |

Complete.

1. 1 mi = ■ ft, so 3 mi = ■ ft
2. 1 mi = ■ yd, so $\frac{1}{2}$ mi = ■ yd
3. 1 c = ■ fl oz, so 7 c = ■ fl oz
4. 4 qt = ■ gal, so 1 qt = ■ gal
5. 1 gal = ■ c
6. 3 pt = ■ fl oz
7. 3 pt = ■ c
8. 2 gal = ■ c
9. 8 oz = ■ lb
10. 1 pt = ■ qt
11. 7 c = ■ pt
12. 36 fl oz = ■ c
13. 5 T = ■ lb
14. 5,000 lb = ■ T

7

Name _____

Math Diagnosis and Intervention System
Intervention Lesson **K4**

Customary Units of Measurement (continued)

Complete.

15. 2 yd = ■ ft
16. 2 yd = ■ in.

17. 4 ft = ■ yd
18. 24 in. = ■ yd

19. 2 gal 1 qt = ■ pt
20. 1 mi 2 yd = ■ ft

21. 18 in. = ■ yd
22. 5 qt = ■ gal

23. 1 gal 1 pt = ■ c
24. 3 qt 1 pt = ■ c

25. 2 qt 1 pt = ■ fl oz
26. 2 yd 2 ft = ■ in.

27. A lot is 180 feet long. A house on this lot is one fourth as long as the lot. What is the length of the house in yards? _____

28. **Math Reasoning** Explain how you would change 4 miles to inches.

_____
_____
_____

29. **Mental Math** 10 gallons is how many quarts? _____

Test Prep Circle the correct letter for the answer.

30. What should you do to change a measurement in miles to a measurement in feet?

   A Multiply by 5,280
   C Multiply by 1,760
   B Divide by 5,280
   D Divide by 1,760

31. Convert $2\frac{1}{2}$ yards to inches.
   A 54 in.   **B** 78 in.   **C** 90 in.   **D** 72 in.

8

Name _____

Intervention Lesson **K5**

Using Metric Units of Length

Example 1

Would you use *centimeters, decimeters, meters,* or *kilometers* to measure the length of a playground?

Think:
The length of a playground is much longer than a centimeter or decimeter. It is shorter than a kilometer. It is most likely several meters long.

Example 2

Find the length of the pencil to the nearest centimeter.

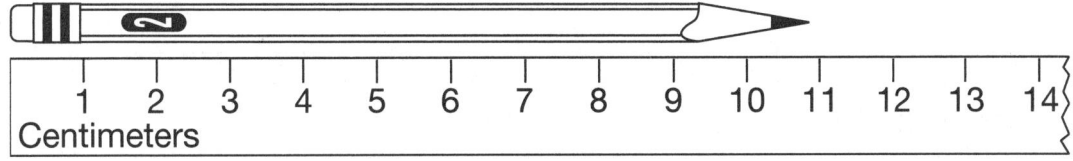

The pencil is longer than 10 centimeters and shorter than 11 centimeters. It is closer to 11 centimeters than it is to 10 centimeters.

To the nearest centimeter, the pencil measures 11 centimeters long.

Estimate each length. Then measure to the nearest centimeter.

1. A sticker

2. A fish

_____   _____

Name _____

Math Diagnosis and Intervention System

Intervention Lesson **K5**

Using Metric Units of Length (continued)

Estimate each length. Then measure to the nearest centimeter.

3.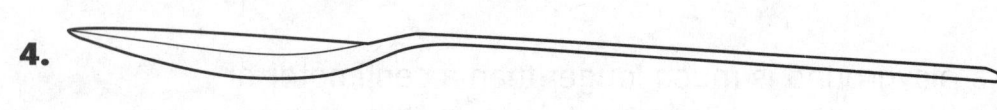

_____

4.

_____

What unit would you use to measure each item?
Write *centimeter*, *decimeter*, *meter*, or *kilometer*.

5. An adult's height

_____

6. Distance traveled on vacation

_____

Choose the best estimate.

7. Length of a car

   5 decimeters or 5 meters

8. Length of a calculator

   12 centimeters or 12 decimeters

Find each missing number.

9. 200 cm = _____ dm

10. 3,000 m = _____ km

11. 4 m = _____ dm

12. 500 cm = _____ m

Test Prep Circle the correct letter for the answer.

13. Which length is NOT equal to the other lengths?

    A 500 centimeters   C 5 meters

    B 5 kilometers   D 50 decimeters

14. Noreen's house is 2 kilometers from school. Which distance is the same as 2 kilometers?

    A 200 centimeters   C 200 decimeters

    B 20 meters   D 2,000 meters

10

Name _____

Intervention Lesson **K6**

Math Diagnosis and Intervention System

Using Customary Units of Capacity

Example 1

Find the missing number: 8 c = ■ pt

Use this information:

2 cups = 1 pint
2 pints = 1 quart
4 quarts = 1 gallon

Since 8 c = 2 c + 2 c + 2 c + 2 c, and 2 c = 1 pt, there are 8 cups in 4 pints. So, 8 c = 4 pt.

Example 2

Find the missing number: 8 pt = ■ gal

Since 8 pt = 2 pt + 2 pt + 2 pt + 2 pt, and 2 pt = 1 qt, there are 4 quarts in 8 pints.

We know 4 qt = 1 gal, so there are 8 pints in 1 gallon.
So, 8 pt = 1 gal.

Find each missing number.

1. 2 pt = _____ c   **2.** 4 c = _____ qt   **3.** 8 qt = _____ gal

4. _____ pt = 6 c   **5.** _____ c = 2 qt   **6.** _____ qt = 3 gal

Choose the best estimate for each container.

7.
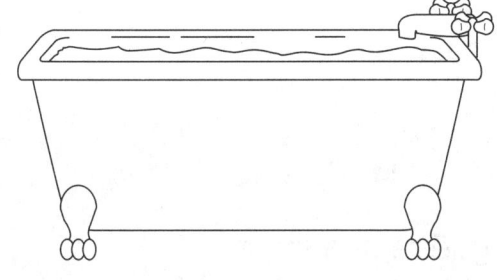

25 c   or   25 gal

8.

2 c   or   2 qt

11

Name _____

Intervention Lesson **K6**

Math Diagnosis and Intervention System

Using Customary Units of Capacity (continued)

Find each missing number.

9. 10 c = _____ pt   10. _____ qt = 1 gal   11. 6 pt = _____ qt

12. _____ gal = 16 qt   13. 4 pt = _____ c   14. _____ qt = 12 c

Choose the best estimate for the capacity of each container.

15.

1 pt or 1 gal

16.

1 c or 1 qt

17. Autumn drinks 6 cups of milk each day. How many pints of milk does she drink each day?

_____

18. Jake is planning to boil some water to make pasta. He will use a pot with a 2-quart capacity. How many cups of water will he need to fill the pot?

_____

19. **Reasoning** If there are 4 quarts in a gallon, how many quarts are in a half-gallon?

_____

Test Prep Circle the correct letter for the answer.

20. Find the missing number: 12 c = pt

   A 1   **B** 2   **C** 4   **D** 6

21. Alicia needs 3 gallons of milk to serve guests at a large dinner. How many quarts does she need?

   A 12 quarts   **B** 8 quarts   **C** 6 quarts   **D** 2 quarts

Name _____

Intervention Lesson **K7**

Using Milliliters and Liters

Example 1

Max wants to find out how much water a rain gauge holds. Should he measure the amount of water the rain gauge holds in milliliters or liters?

Think: A rain gauge holds much more than a medicine dropper, which holds about 1 milliliter, but less than a sports bottle, which holds about 1 liter.

So, Max should measure the amount of water a rain gauge holds in milliliters.

Example 2

Would 8 milliliters or 8 liters be a better estimate for the amount of water a bucket holds?

Think: A bucket holds much more than 8 medicine droppers. It could hold as much as 8 sports bottles.

So, 8 liters is the better estimate.

Choose a unit to measure the capacity of each item. Write *liters* or *milliliters*.

1. A can of soda **2.** A swimming pool **3.** A kitchen sink

_____ _____ _____

Choose the best estimate.

4.

4 L   or   400 mL

5.

6 L   or   650 mL

13

Name _____

Math Diagnosis and Intervention System

Intervention Lesson **K7**

Using Milliliters and Liters (continued)

Choose a unit to measure the capacity of each item. Write *liters* or *milliliters*.

6. A birdbath   **7.** A measuring cup   **8.** A soup bowl

_____   _____   _____

Choose the best estimate.

9.

7 L or 700 mL

10.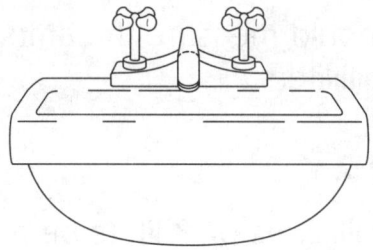

6 L or 60 mL

11. How many milliliters are in a 3-liter soda bottle? _____

12. Kathy bought a 1-liter bottle of soda. She drank 600 milliliters of it yesterday. How many milliliters does she have left? _____

13. Jeff has a 2-liter bottle of water. He drank 750 milliliters of it. How many milliliters does he have remaining? _____

Test Prep Circle the correct letter for the answer.

14. Which measure is the *least*?

  A 3 L   **B** 2 L   **C** 2,300 mL   **D** 3,500 mL

15. Which is the best estimate for the amount of gasoline in a car's gas tank?

  A 45 L   **B** 4 mL   **C** 45 mL   **D** 4 L

Name _____

Intervention Lesson **K8**

Math Diagnosis and Intervention System

Using Ounces and Pounds

Example 1

Compare. Write <, >, or =.

66 oz ● 4 lb

There are 16 ounces in 1 pound.

So, 4 lb = 16 oz + 16 oz + 16 oz + 16 oz = 64 oz.

Since 66 oz > 64 oz, 66 oz > 4 lb.

Example 2

Would 1 oz or 1 lb be a better estimate for the weight of a pencil?

Think:
A football weighs about 1 pound and a key weighs about 1 ounce. A pencil weighs much less than a football, but about the same as a key.

So, 1 oz is a better estimate.

Compare. Write <, >, or =.

1. 15 oz ◯ 1 lb   **2.** 32 oz ◯ 2 lb   **3.** 5 lb ◯ 70 oz

4. 3 lb ◯ 45 oz   **5.** 4 lb ◯ 60 oz   **6.** 1 lb ◯ 18 oz

Choose a unit to measure each item. Write *ounces* or *pounds*.

7. Eyeglasses   **8.** A guitar   **9.** A desk

_____   _____   _____

10. A tomato   **11.** An eraser   **12.** A dog

_____   _____   _____

Using Ounces and Pounds (continued)

Compare. Write <, >, or =.

13. 2 lb ◯ 24 oz   14. 36 oz ◯ 3 lb   15. 12 oz ◯ 1 lb

16. 1 lb ◯ 20 oz   17. 2 lb ◯ 28 oz   18. 48 oz ◯ 3 lb

Choose a unit for each measure. Write *ounces* or *pounds*.

19. A mouse   20. A car   21. A feather

_____   _____   _____

Choose the best estimate.

22. A bowling ball   23. A slice of bread   24. A chicken

    10 oz or 10 lb   1 oz or 1 lb   7 oz or 7 lb

25. A gerbil weighs about 4 ounces. A guinea pig weighs about 1 pound. How much more does a guinea pig weigh than a gerbil? _____

26. A basketball weighs about 22 ounces. A softball weighs about 7 ounces. How much heavier is 1 basketball than 3 softballs? _____

27. A baseball weighs about 5 ounces. A soccer ball weighs about 1 pound. How many baseballs would it take to weigh more than 1 soccer ball? _____

Test Prep Circle the correct letter for the answer.

28. Which of the following weights is equal to 3 pounds?

    A 24 oz   **B** 32 oz   **C** 36 oz   **D** 48 oz

29. A large jar of jelly weighs about 1 pound. A jar of peanut butter weighs about 18 ounces. How much more does the jar of peanut butter weigh than the jar of jelly?

    A 1 oz   **B** 2 oz   **C** 4 oz   **D** 8 oz

Name _____

Math Diagnosis and Intervention System

Intervention Lesson **K9**

Using Grams and Kilograms

Example 1

Compare. Use <, >, or =.

2 kg ● 500 g

You know that there are 1,000 grams in 1 kilogram, so there are 1,000 grams + 1,000 grams = 2,000 grams in 2 kilograms.

Since 2,000 grams is more than 500 grams, 2 kilograms is more than 500 grams. So, 2 kg > 500 g.

Example 2

Would 300 grams or 300 kilograms be a better estimate for how heavy a bag of pretzels is?

Think: A bag of pretzels is heavier than a paper clip but much lighter than a baseball bat.

So, 300 grams is a better estimate.

Compare. Write <, >, or =.

1. 10 kg ◯ 1,000 g **2.** 4 kg ◯ 4,000 g **3.** 500 g ◯ 5 kg

Choose a unit to measure each item. Write *grams* or *kilograms*.

4. car _____ **5.** pencil _____

6. calculator _____ **7.** dog _____

Choose the better estimate.

8.

250 g or 250 kg

9.

5g or 5 kg

17

Name _____

Math Diagnosis and Intervention System
Intervention Lesson **K9**

Using Grams and Kilograms (continued)

Compare. Write <, >, or =.

10. 2,500 g ◯ 2 kg   **11.** 3 kg ◯ 300 g   **12.** 900 g ◯ 1 kg

Choose a unit to measure each item. Write *grams* or *kilograms*.

13. key _____   **14.** hairbrush _____

15. flowerpot _____ **16.** flower _____

Choose the better estimate.

17.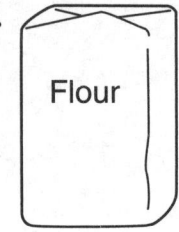

200 g or 2 kg

18.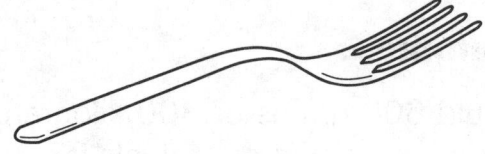

40 g or 4 kg

19. At a party, guests ate 850 grams of corn chips. How many more grams would they need to eat to have eaten 1 kilogram? _____

20. One can of tomato soup weighs 305 grams. How much do 2 cans of soup weigh? _____

21. Reasoning How many more grams is 2 kilograms than 1 kilogram? _____

Test Prep Circle the correct letter for the answer.

22. Which is heaviest?

  A 800 g   **B** 2 kg   **C** 3,000 g   **D** 1 kg

23. Which is the best estimate for the weight of a horse?

  A 700 kg   **B** 7 kg   **C** 1,000 g   **D** 7,000 g

Name _____

Intervention Lesson **K10**

Metric Units of Measurement

Example 1

To change from one metric unit to another, move the decimal point to the right or to the left.

Step 1: Locate the original metric unit on the chart below.

Step 2: Count the number of jumps to the new unit.

Step 3: Move the decimal point as many places as jumps, to the right or to the left.

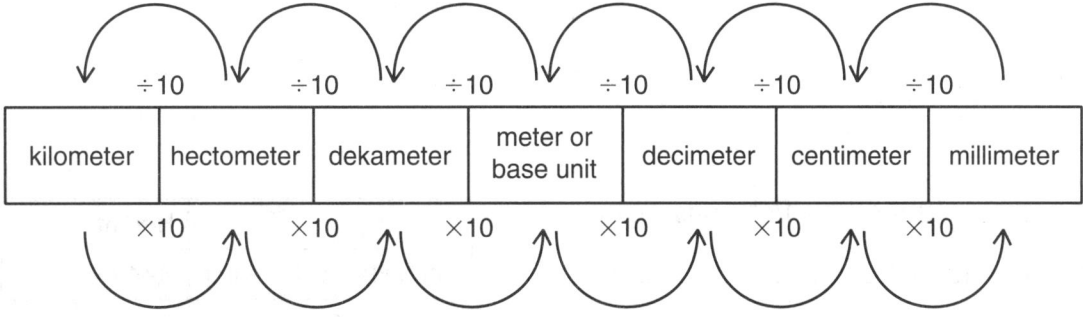

A shipping crate is 3.5 meters long. How many centimeters is this?

It takes 2 jumps to the right to change from meters to centimeters, so move the decimal point 2 places to the right. 3.5 m = 350 cm

Example 2

The height of a door is 198 cm. How many meters is this?

You can rewrite any whole number as a decimal. 198 is the same as 198.0. It takes 2 jumps to the left to change from centimeters to meters, so move the decimal point 2 places to the left. 198.0 cm = 1.98 m

---

Find each equal measure.

1. 742 cm = _____ m

2. 12.4 m = _____ mm

3. 0.62 m = _____ km

4. 35 m = _____ dam

5. 1.7 m = _____ cm

6. 71 hm = _____ m

19

Name _____

Math Diagnosis and Intervention System
Intervention Lesson **K10**

Metric Units of Measurement (continued)

Find each equal measure.

7. 150 mm = _____ cm
8. 2,600 m = _____ km
9. 0.4 dm = _____ mm
10. 3 m = _____ cm
11. 547 cm = _____ m
12. 23 km = _____ m
13. 3.8 km = _____ m
14. 0.2 dm = _____ mm
15. 5 m = _____ cm
16. 79 cm = _____ m
17. 18,000 m = _____ km
18. 22 dam = _____ cm
19. 185 mm = _____ cm
20. 741 cm = _____ m
21. 6.4 km = _____ m

22. What is the height of the Petronas Towers in centimeters? _____

23. What is the height of the CN Tower in meters? _____

Building	Height
John Hancock Center	344 m
Petronas Towers	452 m
Sears Tower	44,200 cm
CN Tower	553,000 mm

24. What is the height of the John Hancock Center in km? _____

25. **Number Sense** Complete the chart with equal measures.

3	km
	dam
	m
	cm

Test Prep Circle the correct letter for the answer.

26. Which measurement is shorter than 15 centimeters?

    A 120 mm   B 0.17 m   C 1 km   D 1 m

27. 18 cm = _____ mm

    A 18   B 180   C 1,800   D 18,000

20

Name _____

Math Diagnosis and Intervention System

Intervention Lesson **K11**

Time to the Quarter-Hour

Example

Look at the clock. Write the hour.
Then write how many minutes
after the hour. Circle the time.

hour 12

minutes 15

1:15      11:15

---

1.  hour _____

   minutes _____

   2:45   3:45   1:45

2.  hour _____

   minutes _____

   4:15   6:15   5:15

3.  hour _____

   minutes _____

   1:45   2:45   3:45

4.  hour _____

   minutes _____

   7:30   8:30   9:30

Name _____

Math Diagnosis and Intervention System

Intervention Lesson **K11**

Time to the Quarter-Hour (continued)

In today's race, one runner starts every 15 minutes. The order of the runners can be told by the numbers on their shirts. Write the name of each runner under the clock that shows when she or he starts running. Then write the time a different way. *Look for the pattern.*

5.

Cora _____   _____   _____   _____

12: 00   12: ____   12: ____   12: ____

6.

_____   _____   _____   _____

1: ____   1: ____   1: ____   1: ____

22

Name _____

Math Diagnosis and Intervention System

Intervention Lesson **K12**

Telling Time

Example

Write the matching time or show it on the clock.

Max wakes up at quarter to __8__.

---

1. Write the time.

   The time is 10 minutes before ____.

2. Draw the hands to show the time.

   "It is quarter to 12."

---

3. Write the time.

   The time is ____ minutes before 3.

4. Draw hands to show the time.

   "It is 6:30."

23

Name _____

Math Diagnosis and Intervention System
Intervention Lesson **K12**

Telling Time (continued)

"I see another way to record the time."

(10 minutes before 4)   10 minutes after 4   11 minutes before 3

Circle the time that matches.

5.    quarter to 6   quarter after 6   quarter to 7

6.    15 minutes after 12   15 minutes before 12   15 minutes before 9

7.    10 minutes before 10   10 minutes before 9   10 minutes after 10

8.    20 minutes before 4   25 minutes before 4   25 minutes before 3

24

Math Diagnosis and Intervention System

Name _____

Intervention Lesson **K13**

Telling Time

Example

Analog clocks have dials and hands. Digital clocks just show numbers.

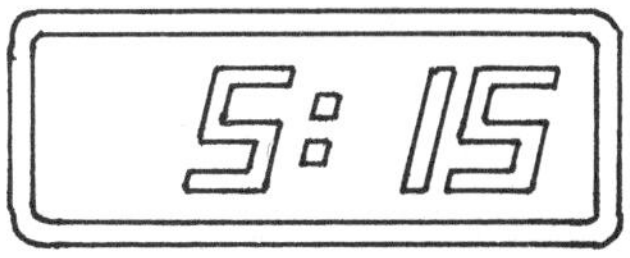

Both clocks here show the time **5:15,** or 15 minutes after 5 o'clock.

We read that as **"five-fifteen."** We can also say **"quarter after five."**

Here are two common ways to say some different times.

Time on the Clock	Way 1	Way 2
6:00 in the morning	Six A.M.	Six o'clock
6:10 in the evening	Six ten P.M.	Ten after six
6:30 in the morning	Six thirty A.M.	Half past six
10:45 in the evening	Ten forty-five P.M.	Quarter to eleven
11:55 in the evening	Eleven fifty-five P.M.	Five to twelve
12:00 mid-day	Twelve P.M.	Noon
12:00 midnight	Twelve A.M.	Midnight

A.M. means morning times from midnight until just before noon.

P.M. means afternoon and evening times from noon until just before midnight.

Write the time shown on each clock in two ways.

1.

2.

25

Name _____

Intervention Lesson **K13**

Telling Time (continued)

Write the time shown on each clock in two ways.

3.

4.

_____

_____

5.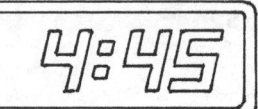

6.

_____

_____

7. Which is a more likely time for a person to eat breakfast, 7:00 A.M. or 7:00 P.M.?

_____

8. **Reasoning** Why might you ask someone to call you at noon instead of 12:00?

_____

_____

_____

Test Prep Circle the correct letter for the answer.

9. Which is the time shown on the clock?

   A quarter to seven   **C** quarter after seven

   B quarter to eight   **D** half past three

Name _____

Intervention Lesson **K14**

Units of Time

To change a smaller unit to a larger unit, you divide.
To change a larger unit to a smaller unit, you multiply.

Example 1

The winning couple at a dance marathon danced for 1,740 minutes. About how many hours was this?

Step 1: Look at the chart. There are 60 minutes in an hour.

Step 2: You are changing a smaller unit (minutes) to a larger unit (hours). So, you divide by 60.
1,740 ÷ 60 = 29 So, the winning couple danced for 29 hours.

Example 2

Fred is two years and ten days older than his brother Ron. How many days is this if a leap year did not occur between their births?

Step 1: Look at the chart. There are 365 days in a year.

Step 2: You are changing a larger unit (years) to a smaller unit (days). So, you multiply by 365.   365 × 2 = 730

Step 3: Add 10 to the number of days you found in Step 2.
730 + 10 = 740

Fred is 740 days older than Ron.

Units of Time
1 minute = 60 seconds
1 hour = 60 minutes
1 day = 24 hours
1 week = 7 days
1 month = about 4 weeks
1 year = 52 weeks
1 year = 12 months
1 year = 365 days
1 leap year = 366 days
1 decade = 10 years
1 century = 100 years
1 millennium = 1,000 years

Write >, <, or = for each ■.

1. 2 years ■ 108 weeks

2. 124 minutes ■ 2 hours

3. 3 centuries ■ 1 millennium

4. 5 years ■ 60 months

Units of Time (continued)

Write >, <, or = for each ■.

5. 2 minutes ■ 126 seconds _____
6. 4 weeks ■ 28 days _____
7. 2 weeks and 3 days ■ 16 days _____
8. 50 weeks ■ 350 days _____
9. 50 hours ■ 2 days _____
10. 208 minutes ■ 4 hours _____
11. 2 decades ■ 34 years _____
12. 28 months ■ 2 years _____
13. 23 weeks ■ 161 days _____
14. 6 hours ■ 150 minutes _____

Find each missing number.

15. 420 seconds = ■ minutes _____
16. 156 weeks = ■ years _____
17. 105 days = ■ weeks _____
18. 3 hours = ■ seconds _____

19. **Number Sense** Which is longer, the number of hours that you sleep a night or the number of hours that you are in school in a day? _____

Test Prep Circle the correct letter for the answer.

20. 198 minutes ■ 4 hours

    A <   B >   C =

21. 4 years = ■ weeks

    A 13   B 48   C 52   D 208

Name _____

Math Diagnosis and Intervention System
Intervention Lesson **K15**

Elapsed Time

Example
Write how many hours have passed.

Kyle started eating lunch at 12 o'clock. He finished at 1 o'clock. It took 1 hour.

Start 12:00

End 1:00

___1___ hour

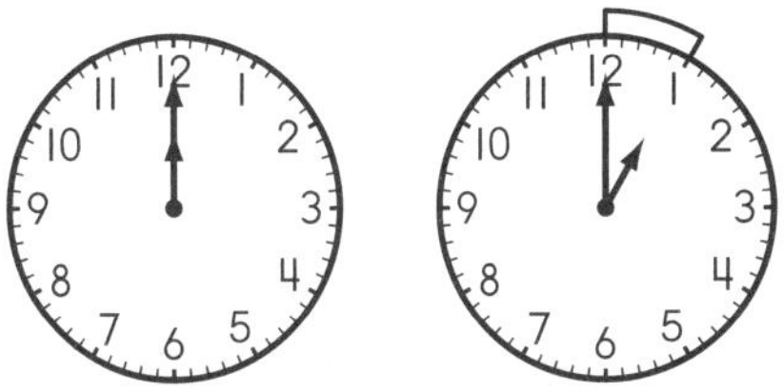

1.

Start _____

End _____

_____ hours

2.

Start _____

End _____

_____ hours

3.

Start _____

End _____

_____ hours

29

Name _____

Intervention Lesson **K15**

Elapsed Time (continued)

Write each end time.

Activity	Starts	Lasts	Ends
4. Pick up toys.	4:30	1 hour	5:30
5. Write a letter.	2:30	30 minutes	_____
6. Play soccer.	10:00	1 hour and 30 minutes	_____
7. Feed a pet.	5:00	15 minutes	_____

30

Name _____

Intervention Lesson **K16**

Elapsed Time; Schedules

Example 1

Connie allows herself 2 hours and 35 minutes to get to the airport and check in before her flight is scheduled to leave. If she leaves her house at 11:15 A.M., what time is her flight?

Step 1: She leaves at 11:15 A.M. Count 2 hours to 1:15 P.M.

Step 2: Count 35 more minutes to 1:50 P.M. Her flight is at 1:50 P.M.

Example 2

Lyle arrived for his doctor's appointment at 2:50 P.M. and waited until 3:14 before the doctor could see him. How long did he sit in the waiting room?

End Time − Start Time = Elapsed Time

Step 1: Write the subtraction as hours and minutes.
  3 h 14 min
− 2 h 50 min

Step 2: Since 14 minutes < 50 minutes, rename 3 h 14 min to 2 h 74 min.

  ~~3 h 14 min~~   2 h 74 min   (60 min = 1 h)
− 2 h 50 min   − 2 h 50 min
                                  24 min

Step 3: Subtract to determine that Lyle waited 24 minutes.

Find each elapsed time.

1. Start: 3:05 A.M.
   Finish: 5:37 A.M.

2. Start: 10:45 A.M.
   Finish: 3:07 P.M.

3. Start: 4:58 P.M.
   Finish: 6:56 P.M.

Name _____

Math Diagnosis and Intervention System

Intervention Lesson **K16**

Elapsed Time; Schedules (continued)

Write the time each clock will show in 38 minutes.

4.

5.

Add or subtract.

6.   6 h 20 min
   − 3 h 40 min

7.   3 h 38 min
   + 6 h 47 min

8. 2 h 39 min
   +   56 min

9.   5 h 10 min
   − 2 h 55 min

10.   5 h 24 min
   + 3 h 41 min

11. 1 h 35 min
   −   56 min

12. **Reasoning** When do you need to change hours to minutes? When do you need to change minutes to hours?

_____

_____

_____

Test Prep Circle the correct letter for the answer.

13. A movie at the theater started promptly at 6:30 P.M. If the movie finished at 8:22 P.M., how long was the movie?

   A 2 h 8 min   C 2 h 12 min

   B 1 h 52 min   D 2 h 58 min

14. An airplane takes off at 6:04 A.M. and lands at 9:37 A.M. How long was the plane in the air?

   A 2 h 33 min   C 2 h 27 min

   B 3 h 41 min   D 3 h 33 min

32

Name _____

Math Diagnosis and Intervention System

Intervention Lesson **K17**

Using a Calendar

Example

You can use the calendar to find days, weeks, and months.

September						
Sunday	Monday	Tuesday	Wednesday	Thursday	Friday	Saturday
			1	2	3	4
5	6	7	8	9	10	11
12	13	14	15	16	17	18
19	20	21	22	23	24	25
26	27	28	29	30		

Ordinal Numbers	Word Form	Months
1st	first	January
2nd	second	February
3rd	third	March
4th	fourth	April
5th	fifth	May
6th	sixth	June
7th	seventh	July
8th	eighth	August
9th	ninth	September
10th	tenth	October
11th	eleventh	November
12th	twelfth	December

1 week = 7 days	12 months = 1 year
52 weeks = 1 year	365 days = 1 year

What is the tenth month of the year?
Look at the table.
Count 10 months, starting with January.
October is the tenth month of the year.

What is the date of the second Saturday in September?
Find the Saturday column in the calendar.
The 4th is the first Saturday of September.
The 11th is the date of the second Saturday.

Use the calendar in the Example to answer Questions 1–4.

1. How many Mondays are there in September? _____

2. What day of the week is September 23rd? _____

3. How many days are there in 2 weeks? _____

4. What date is the second Tuesday of the month? _____

33

Math Diagnosis and Intervention System

Intervention Lesson **K17**

Name _____

Using a Calendar (continued)

April						
Sunday	Monday	Tuesday	Wednesday	Thursday	Friday	Saturday
		1	2	3	4	5
6	7	8	9	10	11	12
13	14	15	16	17	18	19
20	21	22	23	24	25	26
27	28	29	30			

Use the April calendar to answer Questions 5–10.

5. How many days are there in April? _____

6. Which day of the week is April 21st? _____

7. On this calendar, how many Tuesdays are there in April? _____

8. Which date comes right after April 6th? Write an ordinal number. _____

9. Which date is one week from April 4th? _____

10. What date is the third Monday of April? _____

11. Write the ordinal number to describe the month of April when the months of the year are listed in order. _____

12. Reasoning Carol took swimming lessons each day from April 20th to April 24th. Kim took swimming lessons from April 5th to April 11th. How many more lessons did Kim have than Carol? _____

Test Prep Circle the correct letter for the answer.

13. How many months are there in one year?

    A 6 months   **B** 10 months   **C** 11 months   **D** 12 months

14. If January 10th is the second Monday of the month, what is the date of the third Monday of the same month?

    A January 17th   **B** January 24th   **C** January 18th   **D** January 31st

Name _____

Intervention Lesson **K18**

Time Zones

Example

The Earth is divided into 24 time zones.

What time is it in Cairo, Egypt, when it is 4:00 P.M. in London?

7:00 A.M.	12:00 Noon	2:00 P.M.	10:00 P.M.
Wednesday	Wednesday	Wednesday	Wednesday
New York, New York	London, England	Cairo, Egypt	Sydney, Australia

Find the clock for London. Then find the clock for Cairo.

When it is 12:00 noon in London it is 2:00 P.M. in Cairo. So, it is 2 hours later in Cairo than it is in London.

4:00 P.M. + 2 hours = 6:00 P.M.

It is 6:00 P.M. in Cairo when it is 4:00 P.M. in London.

Use the clocks above. Find each time.

1. What time is it in Sydney, Australia, when it is 1:00 P.M. in London?

_____

2. What time is it in London when it is 12:00 P.M. in New York?

_____

3. What time is it in New York when it is 2:00 A.M. in Cairo?

_____

4. What time is it in Cairo when it is 6:00 P.M. in Sydney, Australia?

_____

Name _____

Intervention Lesson **K18**

Time Zones (continued)

Use the clocks below. Find each time.

10:00 A.M.
Friday
Lima, Peru

3:00 P.M.
Friday
Dublin, Ireland

6:00 P.M.
Friday
Nairobi, Kenya

12:00 A.M.
Saturday
Tokyo, Japan

5. What time is it in Nairobi, Kenya, when it is 11:00 A.M. in Dublin?

_____

6. What time is it in Dublin, Ireland, when it is 1:15 P.M. in Tokyo?

_____

Solve.

7. Ottawa, Canada, is two hours behind Buenos Aires, Argentina. What time is it in Ottawa when it is 11:00 A.M. in Buenos Aires? _____

8. **Writing in Math** Sue lives in Lima, Peru. She phoned her friend in Tokyo, Japan. Sue said she was talking on Wednesday, but her friend was talking on Thursday. Is Sue correct? Explain.

_____
_____
_____
_____

Test Prep Use the clocks above. Circle the correct letter for the answer.

9. What is the time in Nairobi when it is 2:00 P.M. in Tokyo?

   A 8:00 P.M.   **B** 2:00 P.M.   **C** 8:00 A.M.   **D** 2:00 A.M.

36

Name _____

Intervention Lesson **K19**

Math Diagnosis and Intervention System

Converting Units

Example 1

How many inches is 4 feet?

Multiply to change larger units into smaller units.

4 ft = ? in.

Think: 1 ft = 12 in.

4 × 12 = 48

4 ft = 48 in.

Customary Units
1 ft = 12 in.
1 yd = 3 ft
1 mi = 5,280 ft
1 c = 8 fl oz
1 pt = 2 c
1 qt = 2 pt
1 gal = 4 qt
1 lb = 16 oz
1 T = 2,000 lb

Example 2

How many meters is 200 centimeters?

Divide to change smaller units into larger units.

200 cm = ? m

Think: 1 m = 100 cm

200 ÷ 100 = 2

200 cm = 2 m

Metric Units
1 cm = 10 mm
1 dm = 10 cm
1 m = 100 cm
1 km = 1,000 m
1 L = 1,000 mL
1 kg = 1,000 g

Find each missing number.

1. 3 pt = _____ c   **2.** 6 lb = _____ oz   **3.** 2 ft 3 in. = _____ in.

4. 21 ft = _____ yd   **5.** 8 qt = _____ gal   **6.** 32 oz = _____ lb

7. 4 km = _____ m   **8.** 20 kg = _____ g   **9.** 600 cm = _____ m

10. 3 L = _____ mL   **11.** 3,000 g = _____ kg   **12.** 5,000 mL = _____ L

© Pearson Education, Inc.

Name _____

Math Diagnosis and Intervention System

Intervention Lesson **K19**

Converting Units (continued)

Find each missing number.

13. 4 c = _____ pt

14. 15 in. = _____ ft _____ in.

15. 6 T = _____ lb

16. 40 oz = _____ lb _____ oz

17. 3 cm = _____ mm

18. 3,400 g = _____ kg _____ g

19. 5,000 mL = _____ L

20. 350 cm = _____ m _____ cm

Solve.

21. Kari bought a box of rice that weighed 2 pounds. How many ounces is that? _____

22. Harrison bought some fruit with a mass of 2 kilograms 300 grams. How many grams is that? _____

23. Carl jogged 4 kilometers around the track. How many meters is that? _____

24. Kendra walked 1 mile 300 feet from her house to the library. How many feet is that? _____

25. Writing in Math Explain how to convert 6 pints to quarts.

_____

_____

Test Prep Circle the correct letter for the answer.

26. 2 T =

    A 100 lb   **C** 2,000 lb

    B 200 lb   **D** 4,000 lb

27. 4,500 g =

    A 45 g   **C** 4 kg 500 g

    B 4 kg   **D** 45 kg

Name _____

Intervention Lesson **K20**

Temperature

Example 1

Look at the thermometer below. What is the temperature in degrees Celsius?

Step 1 Find the Celsius side of the thermometer. Notice that between numbers the marks go up by 1s.

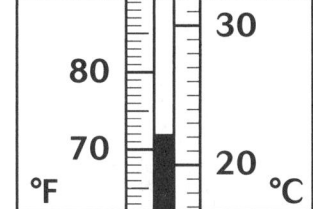

Step 2 Start at 20°C. Then count up by 1s to where the mercury stops.

So, the temperature is 22°C.

Example 2

Which is the better estimate for the temperature of a summer day? 50°F or 80°F

You know that normal room temperature is around 68°F. 50°F is well below 68°F, but 80°F is warmer than room temperature.

So, the better estimate is 80°F.

Choose the better temperature for each activity.

1. bicycle riding
30°F or 70°F

2. camping
0°C or 30°C

3. ice skating
32°F or 72°F

4. wearing shorts
35°C or 100°C

Write each temperature.

5. _____ °C

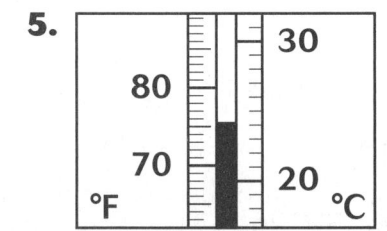

6. _____ °F

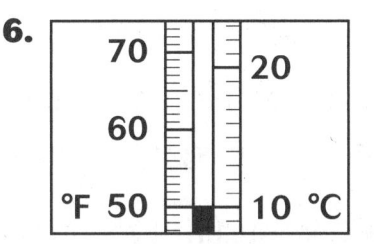

7. _____ °F

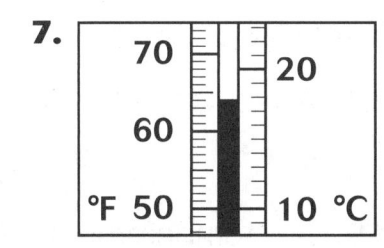

Name _____

Intervention Lesson K20

Temperature (continued)

Choose the better estimate for the temperature.

8. hot pizza
80°F or 160°F

9. ice cream
0°C or 30°C

10. bathwater
45°F or 95°F

11. cold drink
0°C or 10°C

Write each temperature.

12. _____ °F

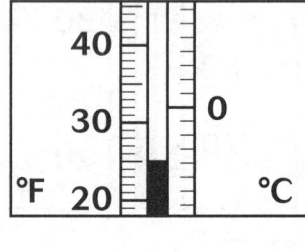

13. _____ °C

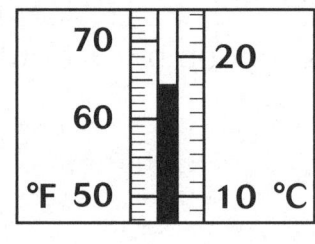

14. _____ °F

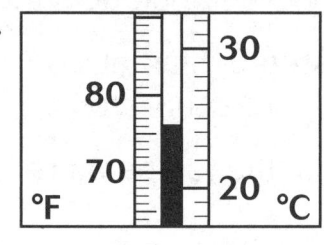

15. One cold morning, the temperature was 35°F. The temperature rose to 53°F later in the day. How many degrees had the temperature increased? _____

16. This morning the temperature was 65°F. Then it rose 3°. Then the temperature dropped 10°. What was the final temperature? _____

17. Writing in Math Joe thinks that 0°C is the same as 32°F. Do you agree? Why?

_____

_____

Test Prep Circle the correct letter for the answer.

18. Which is the best estimate for the temperature of cold milk?

A 0°F   B 25°F   C 34°F   D 80°F

19. The temperature is 33°C in Austin, 12°C in Summit, 5°C in Atlanta, and 18°C in Meyersville. In which city could you swim outdoors?

A Austin   B Summit   C Atlanta   D Meyersville

40

Name _____

Intervention Lesson **K21**

Temperature

Example 1

Find the temperature shown on the thermometer in degrees Fahrenheit and degrees Celsius.

Using customary units, the temperature is 68 degrees Fahrenheit, or 68° F.

Using metric units, the temperature is 20 degrees Celsius, or 20°C.

This is the standard room temperature.

Example 2

Which temperature is cooler, ⁻10°C or ⁻10°F?

You can use the thermometer to compare these temperatures.

Since ⁻10°F is lower on the thermometer than ⁻10°C, ⁻10°F is the lower temperature.

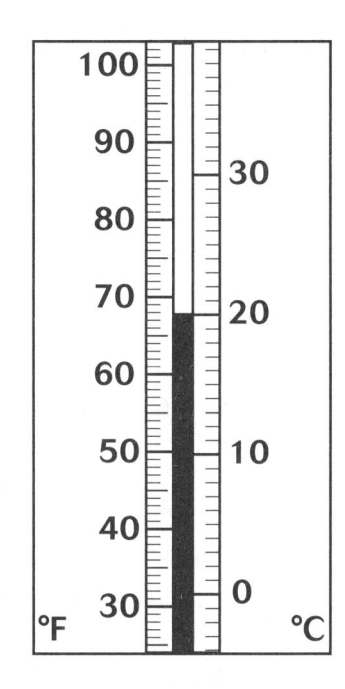

Use the thermometer above to write the equivalent temperature in degrees Fahrenheit or degrees Celsius.

1. 59°F **2.** 25°C **3.** ⁻2°C **4.** 46°F

_____ _____ _____ _____

5. 41°F **6.** 38°C **7.** 72°F **8.** 8°C

_____ _____ _____ _____

9. 29°C **10.** 50°F **11.** 39°C **12.** 86°F

_____ _____ _____ _____

41

Name _____

Intervention Lesson **K21**

Temperature (continued)

Use the thermometer on page 41. Write the equivalent temperature in degrees Fahrenheit or degrees Celsius.

13. 30°C **14.** 32°F **15.** 35°C **16.** 95°F

17. 64°F **18.** 36°F **19.** 15°C **20.** −2°C

Choose the most appropriate temperature in Exercises 21–24. The table at the right provides some information that may be helpful.

	°F	°C
Water boils	212	100
Normal body temperature	98.6	37
Room temperature	68	20
Water freezes	32	0

21. hot coffee
70°F or 70°C

22. cold milk
0°F or 4°C

23. a warm day
75°F or 75°C

24. a cool day
5°F or 10°C

Read each thermometer. Write the temperature in °F or °C.

25. **26.** **27.** **28.**

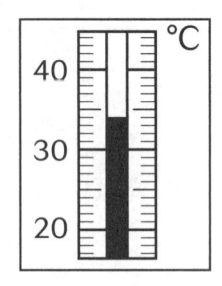

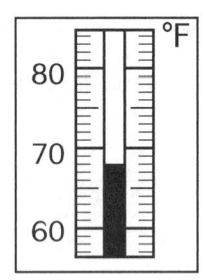

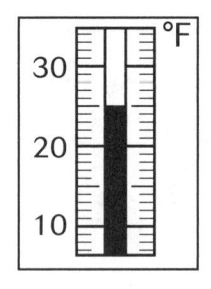

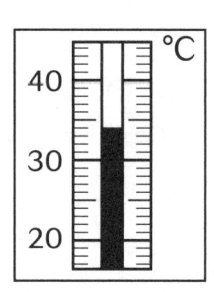

Test Prep Circle the correct letter for the answer.

29. Using the thermometer at the right, which temperature is equivalent to 46°F?

A 4°C **C** 8°C

B 6°C **D** 10°C

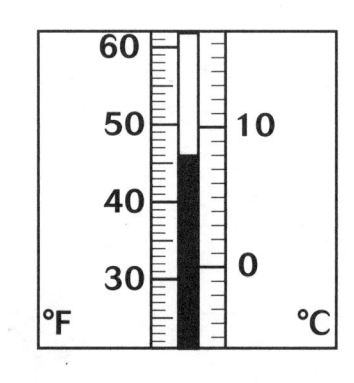

Intervention Lesson **K22**

Units of Measure and Precision

Example

Use a ruler marked in inches to measure objects to the nearest inch, $\frac{1}{2}$ inch, $\frac{1}{4}$ inch, $\frac{1}{8}$ inch, or $\frac{1}{16}$ inch.

Rulers marked in centimeters can be used to measure items to the nearest centimeter or millimeter.

The smaller the units on the scale of a measuring device, the more **precise** the measurement is.

What is the length of the crayon to the nearest whole, half, quarter, eighth, and sixteenth inch? What is the length to the nearest centimeter and millimeter?

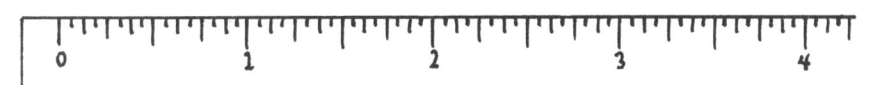

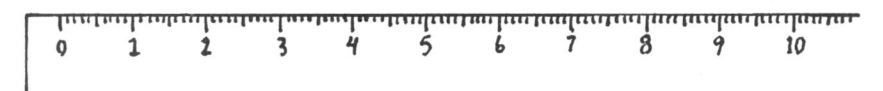

The length of the crayon to the nearest:

whole inch ___2___   half inch ___2___   quarter inch ___$2\frac{1}{4}$___

eighth inch ___$2\frac{1}{8}$___   sixteenth inch ___$2\frac{2}{16}$___

centimeter ___5 or 6___   millimeter ___55___

Measure each line segment to the nearest $\frac{1}{8}$ inch and nearest centimeter.

1. ─────────────────   **2.** ─────

43

Units of Measure and Precision (continued)

Measure each object to the nearest $\frac{1}{8}$ inch and nearest centimeter.

3. _____

4. _____

Measure each line segment to the nearest $\frac{1}{16}$ inch and nearest millimeter.

5. _____

6. _____

7. _____

Use your ruler to draw a line segment of each length.

8. $\frac{3}{8}$ in.

9. $5\frac{3}{4}$ in.

10. $2\frac{3}{16}$ in.

11. 7 cm

12. 85 mm

13. 102 mm

14. **Number Sense** Will a ruler marked in $\frac{1}{2}$ inch units or one marked in centimeters give a more precise measurement?

_____

_____

Test Prep Circle the correct letter for the answer.

15. Which measurement of the object is the most precise?
   _____

   A 40 cm   **B** 35 mm   **C** 30 cm   **D** 40 mm

Name _____

Intervention Lesson **K23**

Converting Between Measurement Systems

Example 1

Use the equivalent at the right to convert $\frac{3}{4}$ meter to inches.

0.75 m = ■ in.

1 m ≈ 39.97 in.

0.75 × 39.97 ≈ 29.9775

0.75 m ≈ 29.98 in.

Example 2

Andy's Supermart sells root beer in 3-liter bottles for $1.29. About how many gallons of root beer are contained in a 3-liter bottle?

3 L ≈ ■ gal

1 gal ≈ 3.79 L

3 ÷ 3.79 ≈ 0.79

3 L ≈ 0.79 gal

Customary and Metric Unit Equivalent

Length
1 in. = 2.54 cm
1 m ≈ 39.97 in.
1 m ≈ 1.09 yd
1 mi ≈ 1.61 km

Weight and Mass
1 oz ≈ 28.35 g
1 kg ≈ 2.2 lb
1 metric ton (t) ≈ 1.102 tons (T)

Capacity
1 L ≈ 1.06 qt
1 gal ≈ 3.79 L

Complete. Round to the nearest tenth, if necessary.

1. 3.8 m ≈ ■ in.

_____

2. 50 g ≈ ■ oz

_____

3. 90 yd ≈ ■ m

_____

4. 44 in. ≈ ■ cm

_____

5. 2.5 t ≈ ■ T

_____

6. $3\frac{1}{2}$ kg ≈ ■ lb

_____

7. $5\frac{1}{4}$ qt ≈ ■ L

_____

8. 100 km ≈ ■ mi

_____

9. 10 cm ≈ ■ in.

_____

45

Name _____

Intervention Lesson **K23**

Converting Between Measurement Systems (continued)

Complete. Round to the nearest tenth, if necessary.

10. 2 cm ≈ ■ in.   **11.** 2.4 t ≈ ■ T   **12.** $8\frac{2}{3}$ m ≈ ■ yd

_____   _____   _____

13. $3\frac{1}{2}$ yd ≈ ■ m   **14.** 500 lb ≈ ■ kg   **15.** 11 in. ≈ ■ m

_____   _____   _____

16. 38 in. ≈ ■ cm   **17.** 3 L ≈ ■ gal   **18.** 7.2 T ≈ ■ t

_____   _____   _____

19. A necklace measures $16\frac{1}{2}$ inches. About how many centimeters is this? _____

20. Rewrite the materials list at the right using meters for fabric, inches for thread, and kilograms for stuffing. Write your conversions in the following spaces:

Materials List
$1\frac{1}{2}$ yd fabric
65 cm thread
$1\frac{3}{4}$ lb stuffing

fabric: _____ m   thread: _____ in.   stuffing: _____ kg

21. Mental Math Use < and > to determine which length is longer.

  a. 2 cm ● 1 in.   **b.** 1 mi ● 1 km   **c.** 1 yd ● 1 m

  _____   _____   _____

Test Prep Circle the correct letter for the answer.

22. 5 gallons is about _____ L.

  A 0.8   **B** 19   **C** 12   **D** 5

23. 1.27 centimeters = _____ in.

  A $\frac{2}{3}$ **B** $\frac{1}{2}$ **C** $\frac{1}{4}$ **D** 2

Name _____

Intervention Lesson **K24**

Math Diagnosis and Intervention System

Perimeter

Example 1

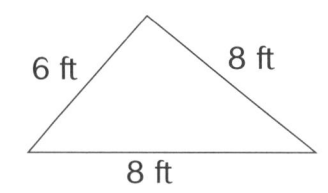

Find the perimeter of the triangle at the right.

Add the lengths of the sides.

6 + 8 + 8 = 22

So, the perimeter of the triangle is 22 feet.

Example 2

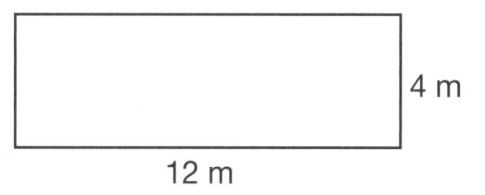

Find the perimeter of the rectangle at the right.

You know that opposite sides of a rectangle have the same length. So, there are two sides with length 12 meters and two sides with length 4 meters.

Add all the lengths.

12 + 4 + 12 + 4 = 32

The perimeter of the rectangle is 32 meters.

Find the perimeter of each figure.

1. 3 in., 5 in., 4 in.

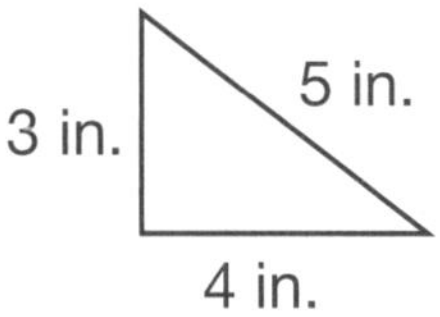

2. 5 cm, 1 cm, 5 cm, 1 cm

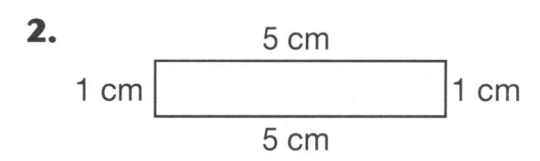

3. 9 cm (square)

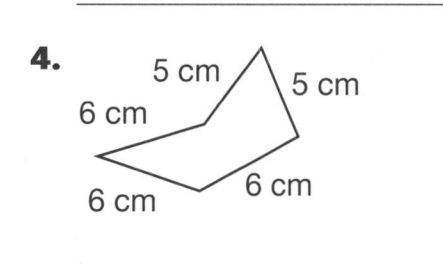

4. 5 cm, 5 cm, 6 cm, 6 cm, 6 cm

47

Name _____

Intervention Lesson K24

Perimeter (continued)

Find the perimeter of each figure.

5. 16 ft / 2 ft / 2 ft / 16 ft

_____

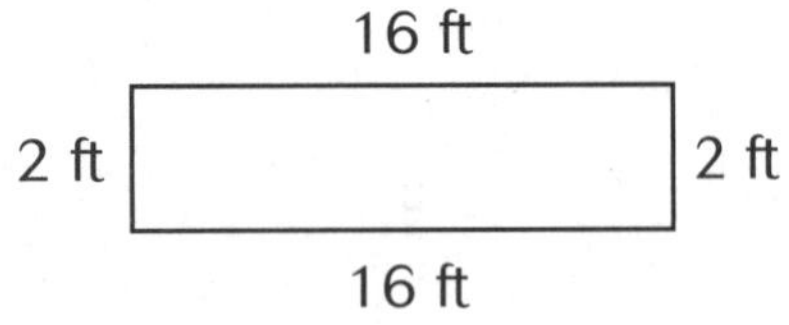

6. 4 in. / 2 in. / 6 in.

_____

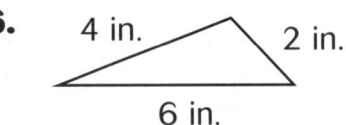

7. 4 in. (square)

_____

8. 7 cm / 4 cm / 6 cm / 5 cm / 2 cm

_____

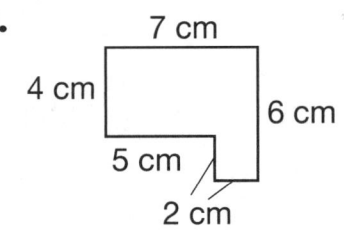

9. Trevor is making a pen for his pet rabbits. His pen is 8 feet long and 6 feet wide. How many feet of fencing will Trevor need? _____

10. Tom is making a square garden with sides 10 feet long. How many feet of fencing will he need? _____

Test Prep Circle the correct letter for the answer.

11. Which is the perimeter of the square?
    A 2 inches
    B 4 inches
    C 8 inches
    D 12 inches

    2 in.

12. Which is the perimeter of the triangle?
    A 3 cm
    B 6 cm
    C 9 cm
    D 15 cm

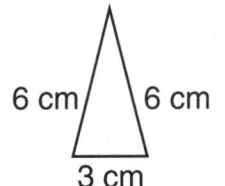

    6 cm / 6 cm / 3 cm

Name _____

Intervention Lesson **K25**

Area

Example 1

Find the area of the rectangle on the grid paper.

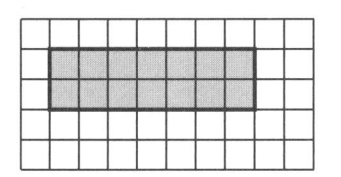

Each square on the grid paper is one square unit. The number of shaded squares is the area of the rectangle.

Since there are 14 shaded squares, the area is 14 square units.

Example 2

Estimate the area of each figure. Which has the largest area?

Count two partly covered squares as one whole square to estimate the area.

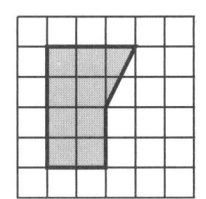

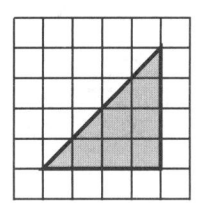

There are 8 whole squares and 2 partly covered squares. The area is about 9 square units.

There are 6 whole units and 4 partly covered squares. The area is about 8 square units.

The first figure has the largest area.

Find each area. Write your answer in square units.

1.

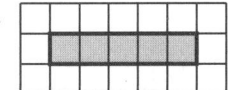

2.

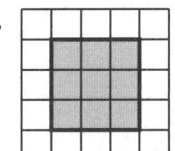

3.

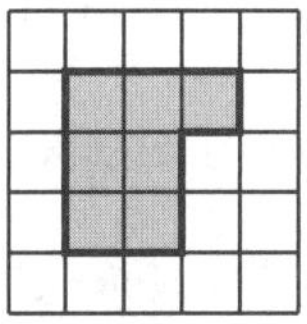

_____   _____   _____

_____   _____   _____

49

Name _____

Intervention Lesson **K25**

Area (continued)

Find each area. Write your answer in square units.

4.

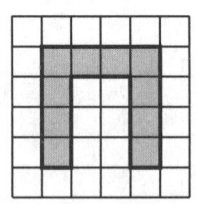

5.

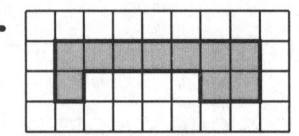

6.

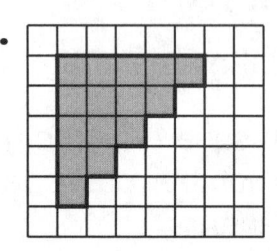

Judy baked several different shapes of cookies and wants to know which is largest. Each cookie was placed on a grid. Estimate the area of each cookie in Exercises 7–9.

7. Triangle

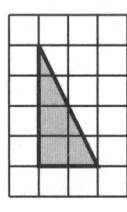

8. Hexagon

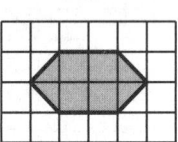

9. Quadrilateral

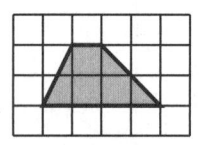

10. Which cookie in Exercises 7–9 was the largest?

Test Prep Circle the correct letter for the answer.

11. What is the area of this figure?

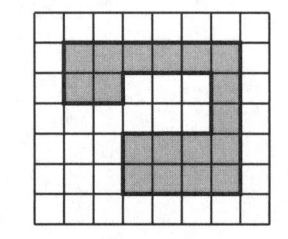

   A 16 square units   **C** 19 square units

   B 18 square units   **D** 20 square units

Intervention Lesson **K26**

Perimeter

Example

Find the perimeter of the figure at the right.

Perimeter = 7 cm + 12 cm + 5 cm + 5 cm
            = 29 cm

The perimeter of the figure is 29 centimeters.

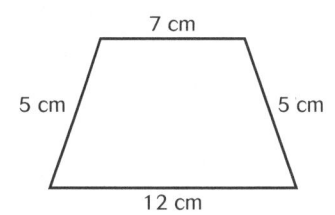

Find the perimeter of each figure.

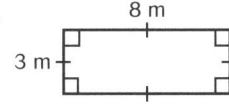

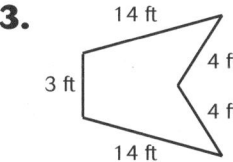

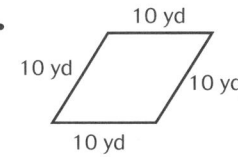

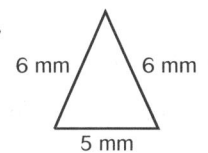

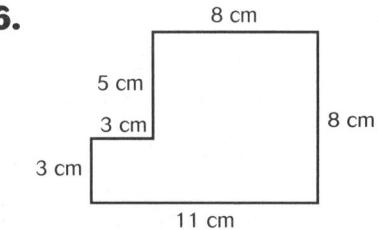

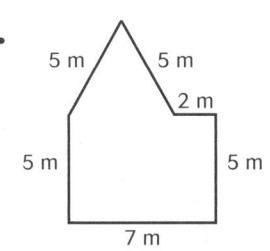

1. 7 in. square (7 in. on each side)

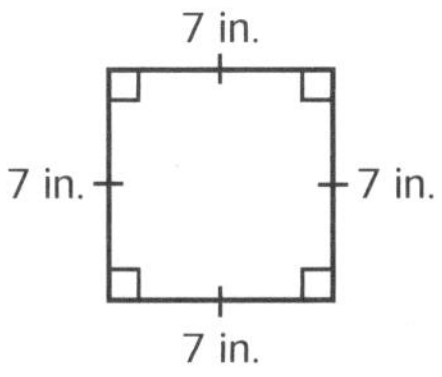

_____

2. 8 m by 3 m rectangle

_____

3. 14 ft, 4 ft, 4 ft, 14 ft, 3 ft

_____

4. parallelogram with sides 10 yd, 10 yd, 10 yd, 10 yd

_____

5. triangle with sides 6 mm, 6 mm, 5 mm

_____

6. 8 cm, 5 cm, 3 cm, 3 cm, 11 cm, 8 cm

_____

7. 5 m, 5 m, 2 m, 5 m, 7 m, 5 m

_____

8. pentagon with all sides 12 in.

_____

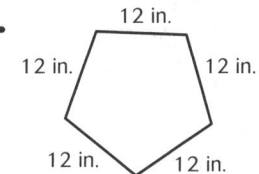

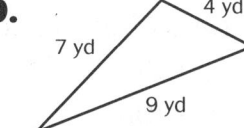

9. triangle with sides 4 yd, 7 yd, 9 yd

_____

51

Name _____

Intervention Lesson K26

Perimeter (continued)

Find the perimeter of the rectangle with the given dimensions.

10. $l = 9$ mm, $w = 12$ mm _____

11. $l = 13$ in., $w = 14$ in. _____

12. $l = 2$ ft, $w = 15$ ft _____

13. $l = 17$ cm, $w = 25$ cm _____

14. $l = 42$ m, $w = 30$ m _____

15. $l = 1$ yd, $w = 14$ yd _____

Find the perimeter of the square with the given side.

16. $s = 2$ yd _____

17. $s = 10$ in. _____

18. $s = 31$ km _____

19. $s = 11$ m _____

20. The perimeter of a rhombus is 52 millimeters. What is the length of each side? _____

21. A rectangle has a perimeter of 70 hectometers. The width of the rectangle is 14 hectometers. Find the length of the rectangle. _____

22. An equilateral triangle has a perimeter of 153 feet. What is the length of each side? _____

23. Mariah has a rectangular garden. The garden is twice as long as it is wide. If the perimeter of the garden is 84 meters, find the rectangle's dimensions. _____

Test Prep Circle the correct letter for the answer.

24. Find the perimeter of a rectangle with a length of 16 yards and a width of 4 yards.

   A 20 yd   **B** 24 yd   **C** 30 yd   **D** 40 yd

Circumference

Find the circumference of each circle below to the nearest whole number.
Use 3.14 or $\frac{22}{7}$ for π.

Example 1

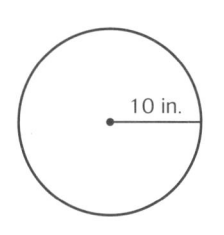

$C = 2\pi r$

$C \approx 2 \times 3.14 \times 10$

$C \approx 62.8$

10 in.

The circumference is about 63 inches.

Example 2

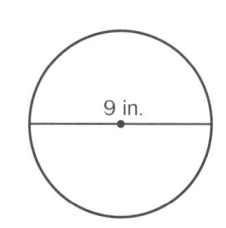

$C \approx \pi d$

$C \approx 3.14 \times 9$

$C \approx 28.26$

9 in.

The circumference is about 28 inches.

Find the circumference of each circle to the nearest whole number.
Use 3.14 or $\frac{22}{7}$ for π.

1. 12 m

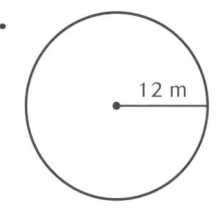

2. 14 ft

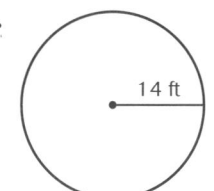

3. 16 cm

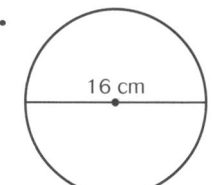

4. 28 yd

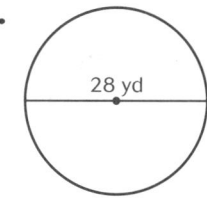

5. 2 in.

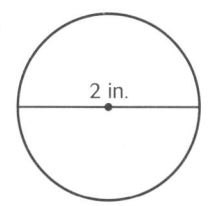

6. 13 mm

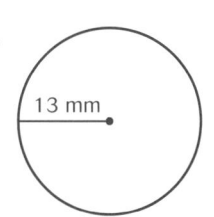

7. 15 ft

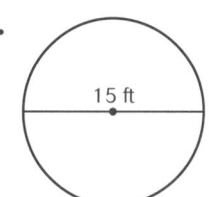

8. 35 m

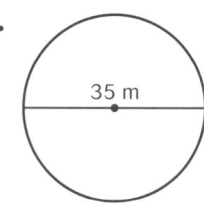

9. 3.6 cm

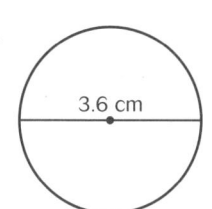

10. 5.7 yd

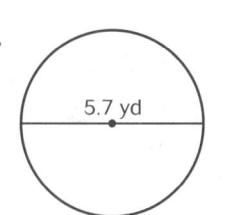

11. $1\frac{1}{2}$ in.

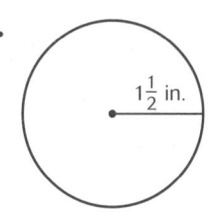

12. 9.7 ft

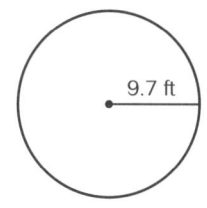

Name _____

Intervention Lesson **K27**

Circumference (continued)

Find the circumference of each circle. Use 3.14 or $\frac{22}{7}$ for π.

13. 17.5 m

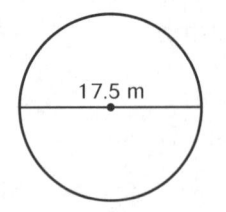

14. $22\frac{1}{2}$ cm

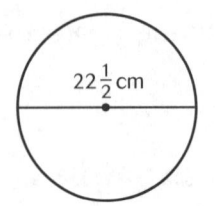

15. 42 ft

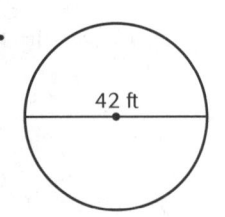

16. 17.5 yd

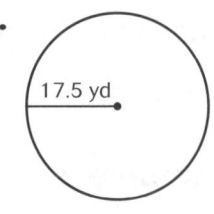

_____ _____ _____ _____

17. 13.7 in.

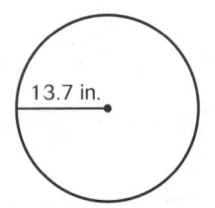

18. 100 mm

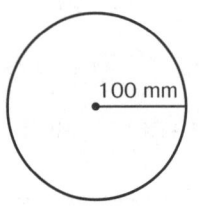

19. $27\frac{1}{2}$ ft

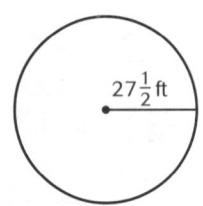

20. $43\frac{1}{2}$ m

_____ _____ _____ _____

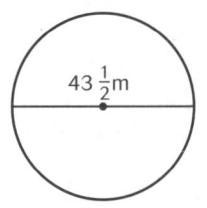

21. Find the circumference of a circle with a radius of $4\frac{1}{2}$ yards. Round your answer to the nearest whole number. _____

22. Number Sense Find the distance around the figure at the right. Round your answer to the nearest whole number.

4 in.
8 in.   8 in.
4 in.

_____

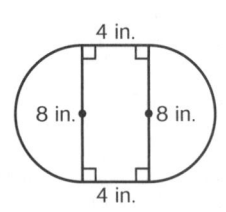

23. Math Reasoning Write a formula for the circumference (C) of a semicircle.

_____

Test Prep Circle the correct letter for the answer.

24. Find the circumference of the circle at the right to the nearest whole number.

  A 15 m   **B** 60 m   **C** 30 m   **D** 9.6 m

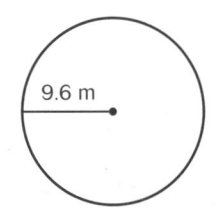

9.6 m

25. Find the circumference of a circle with a radius of $20\frac{1}{2}$ feet.

  A 128.74 ft   **B** 65.94 ft   **C** 31.37 ft   **D** 41.06 ft

Name _____

Intervention Lesson **K28**

Area

Example 1

Find the area of a rectangle.

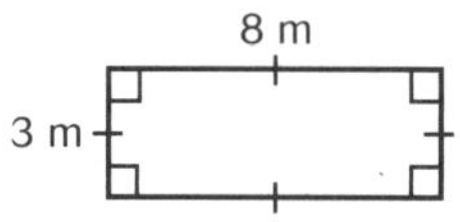

8 m, 3 m

$A = l \times w$

$A = 8\ m \times 3\ m$ ← $l = 8, w = 3$

$A = 24$ square meters

The area of the rectangle is 24 m².

Example 2

Find the area of a parallelogram.

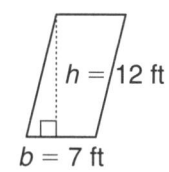

$h = 12$ ft, $b = 7$ ft

$A = b \times h$

$A = 7\ ft \times 12\ ft$ ← $b = 7, h = 12$

$A = 84$ square feet

The area of the parallelogram is 84 ft².

Find the area of each figure.

1. 7 in., 7 in., 7 in.

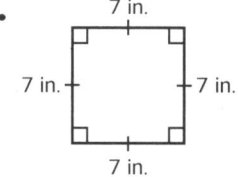

2. 5 cm, 3 cm

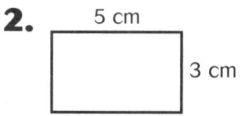

3. 20 m, 15 m

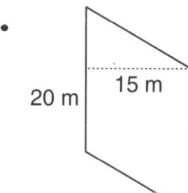

4. 2 ft, 7 ft

5. 8 hm, 10 hm

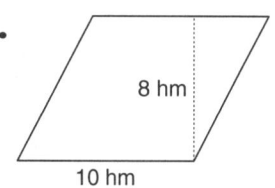

6. 12 yd, 12 yd, 12 yd, 12 yd

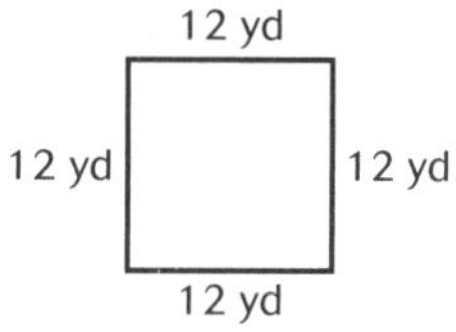

7. 2 km, 14 km

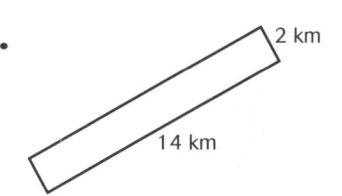

8. 7 in., 11 in.

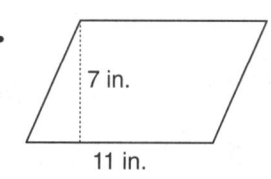

9. 13 m, 13 m, 13 m, 13 m

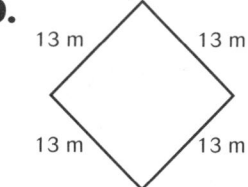

Name _____

Math Diagnosis and Intervention System

Intervention Lesson **K28**

Area (continued)

Find the area of each figure.

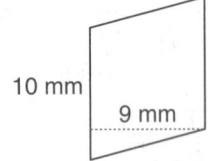

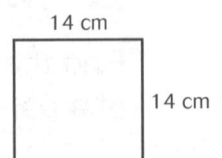

10. 10 mm, 9 mm

11. 14 cm, 14 cm

12. 12 ft, 15 ft

_____   _____   _____

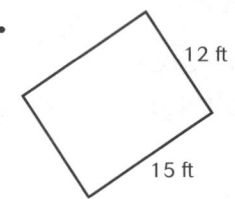

Find the area of the rectangle with the given dimensions.

13. $l = 15$ mm, $w = 4$ mm

14. $l = 3$ cm, $w = 10$ cm

_____   _____

15. $l = 12$ in., $w = 5$ in. _____

Find the area of the square with the given side length.

16. $s = 16$ cm

17. $s = 30$ m

18. $s = 1$ ft

_____   _____   _____

19. The area of a parallelogram is 100 square millimeters. The length is 4 millimeters. Find the height. _____

20. The area of a square is 81 square feet. What is the length of each side? _____

21. Number Sense Using only whole numbers, what are the possible dimensions of a rectangle with an area of 12 square centimeters?

_____

Test Prep Circle the correct letter for the answer.

22. Find the area of a square with a side length of 17 meters.

A 289 m^2 B 34 m^2 C 68 m^2 D 145 m^2

Name _____

Intervention Lesson **K29**

Area

Example 1

Find the area of this parallelogram.

$A = b \times h$

$A = 9 \times 5$

$A = 45 \text{ m}^2$

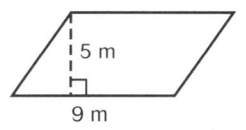

Example 2

Find the area of this triangle.

$A = \frac{1}{2} \times b \times h$

$A = \frac{1}{2} \times 6 \times 3$

$A = \frac{1}{2} \times 18$

$A = 9 \text{ in.}^2$

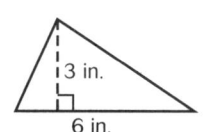

Find the area of each figure.

1. 27 ft, 13 ft

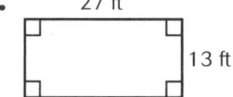

2. 5.9 km, 5.9 km

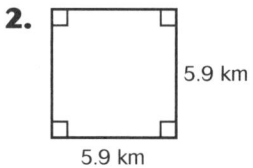

3. 1.5 in., 2 in., 5 in.

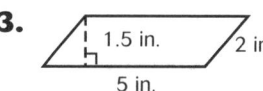

4. 6 cm, 7 cm

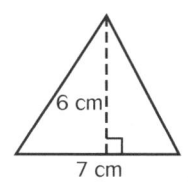

5. 5 ft, 10 ft

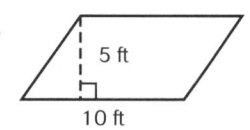

6. 4 m, 11 m

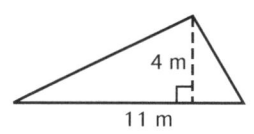

7. 7 in., 16 in.

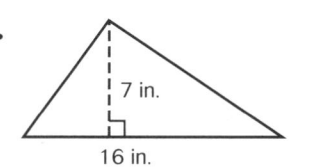

8. 9 m, 3.1 m

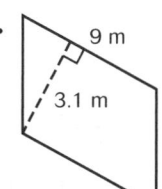

9. 15 yd, 9 yd, 12 yd

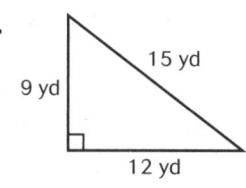

57

Name _____

Math Diagnosis and Intervention System

Intervention Lesson **K29**

Area (continued)

Find the missing measurement.

10. rectangle
$l = 2.8$ ft
$w = 5$ ft
$A = $ ■

11. rectangle
$A = 465$ in.^{2}
$l = 15$ in.
$w = $ ■

12. square
$s = 5\frac{1}{2}$ m
$A = $ ■

13. square
$A = 81$ cm^2
$s = $ ■

14. triangle
$b = 22$ yd
$h = 20$ yd
$A = $ ■

15. parallelogram
$A = 42$ km^2
$b = 7$ km
$h = $ ■

16. parallelogram
$b = 13.7$ ft
$h = 7.1$ ft
$A = $ ■

17. triangle
$A = 16$ mm^2
$b = 8$ mm
$h = $ ■

18. Brett is carpeting a 4-yard by 3-yard room. If carpet sells for $24.95 per square yard, how much will Brett pay for carpet? _____

19. Math Reasoning Tiles sell for $1.50 per tile. Each tile is one square foot. What are the dimensions of the largest square area that can be tiled for $100.00? _____

Test Prep Circle the correct letter for the answer.

20. Find the area of the triangle.

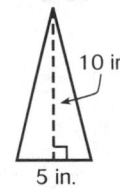

A 23 in.^{2} **C** 15 in.^{2}
B 112 in.^{2} **D** 25 in.^{2}

10 in.
5 in.

21. The area of a parallelogram is 75 cm^2 and its height is 6 cm. Find the length of the base.

A 12.5 cm   **C** 25 cm
B 6.25 cm   **D** 11 cm

58

Name _____

Intervention Lesson **K30**

Math Diagnosis and Intervention System

Areas of Irregular Figures

Example

Find the area of the irregular figure at the right.

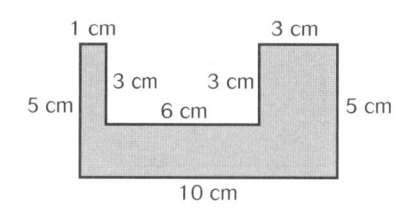

First, divide the figure into three rectangles. Then, add the areas together.

You know the formula used to find the area of a rectangle, $A = l \times w$, where l is the length of the rectangle and w is the width.

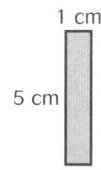

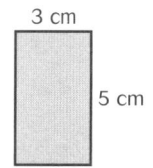

$A = l \times w$	$A = l \times w$	$A = l \times w$
$A = 5 \text{ cm} \times 1 \text{ cm}$	$A = 6 \text{ cm} \times 2 \text{ cm}$	$A = 5 \text{ cm} \times 3 \text{ cm}$
$A = 5 \text{ square cm}$	$A = 12 \text{ square cm}$	$A = 15 \text{ square cm}$

Total area = 5 square cm + 12 square cm + 15 square cm

= 32 square cm or 32 cm^2

Find the area of each irregular figure.

1.

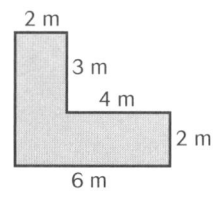

2.

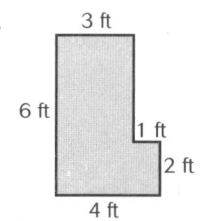

3.

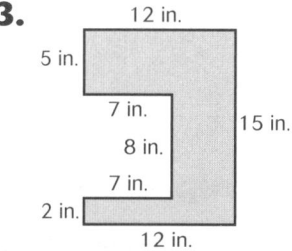

_____   _____   _____

© Pearson Education, Inc.

59

Name _____

Intervention Lesson **K30**

Math Diagnosis and Intervention System

Areas of Irregular Figures (continued)

Find the area of each irregular figure.

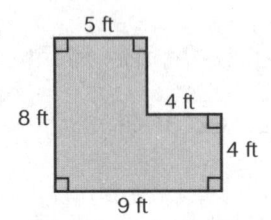

4. (figure: 15 m top, 8 m, 7 m, 7 m, 15 m left, 22 m bottom)

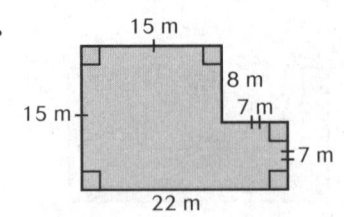

5. (figure: 5 ft top, 4 ft, 8 ft left, 4 ft, 9 ft bottom)

6. (figure: 6 cm, 4 cm, 5 cm, 4 cm, 10 cm)

_____   _____   _____

7. (figure: 3 in., 6 in., 11 in., 3 in., 4 in.)

8. (figure: 5 m, 5 m, 8 m, 6 m, 20 m, 20 m, 8 m, 5 m, 5 m)

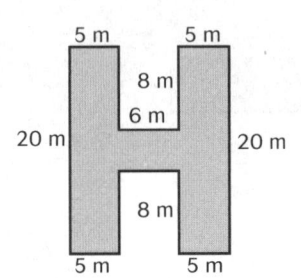

9. (figure: 4 yd, 6 yd, 6 yd, 10 yd, 4 yd, 15 yd)

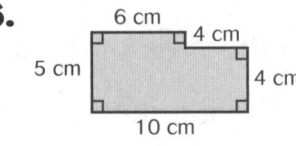

_____   _____   _____

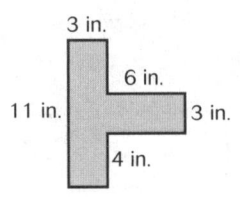

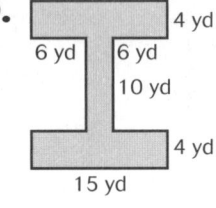

Use the figure at the right for Exercises 10 and 11.

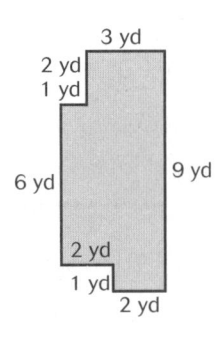

(figure: 3 yd, 2 yd, 1 yd, 6 yd, 9 yd, 2 yd, 1 yd, 2 yd)

10. Bob wants to carpet the room shown. How many square yards of carpet will he need?

_____

11. If the carpet costs $21.95 per square yard, how much will it cost to carpet the room?

_____

Test Prep Circle the correct letter for the answer.

12. Jacob wants to tile the room shown at the right. What is the area of the room?

    A 124 ft^2 **C** 153 ft^2

    B 144 ft^2 **D** 184 ft^2

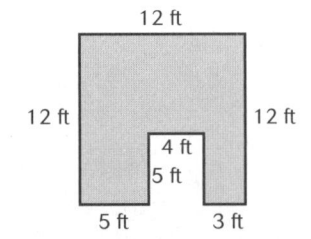

(figure: 12 ft top, 12 ft left, 12 ft right, 4 ft, 5 ft, 5 ft, 3 ft)

Name _____

Math Diagnosis and Intervention System

Intervention Lesson **K31**

Rectangles with the Same Area

Example

Draw all the different rectangular shapes with an area of 16 square meters. Then, find the perimeter of each rectangle.

You know the formula for the area of a rectangle is $A = l \times w$ and the formula for the perimeter of a rectangle is $P = 2l + 2w$.

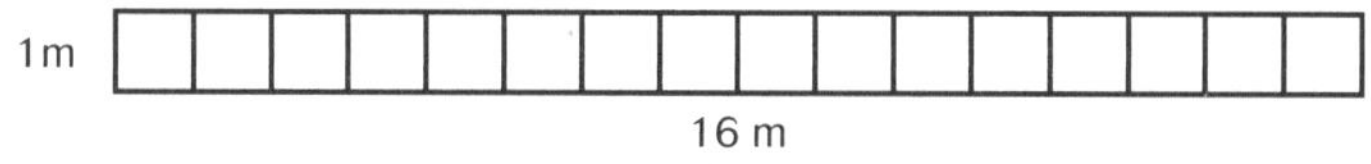

1 m × 16 m rectangle

$A = 16 \times 1 = 16 \text{ m}^2$
$P = 2 \times 16 + 2 \times 1 = 34 \text{ m}$

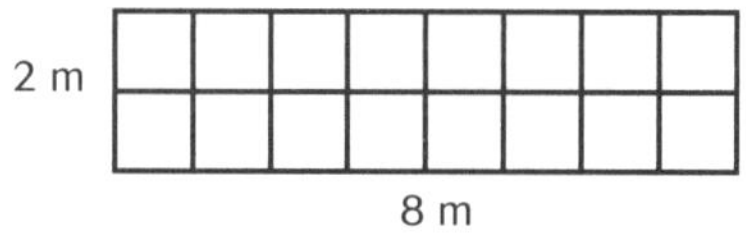

2 m × 8 m rectangle

$A = 8 \times 2 = 16 \text{ m}^2$
$P = 2 \times 8 + 2 \times 2 = 20 \text{ m}$

4 m × 4 m rectangle

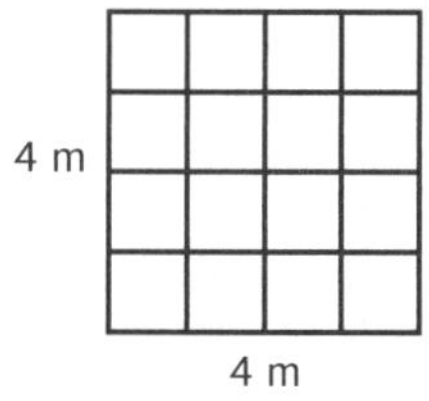

$A = 4 \times 4 = 16 \text{ m}^2$
$P = 2 \times 4 + 2 \times 4 = 16 \text{ m}$

Each rectangle has an area of 16 square meters. The perimeters of the rectangles are 34 m, 20 m, and 16 m.

Draw a rectangle with the same area as the one shown. Then find the perimeter of each.

1. $P = 12$ in.
2 in. × 4 in.

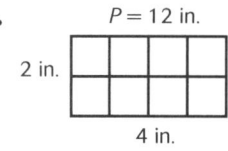

2. $P = 18$ cm
3 cm × 6 cm

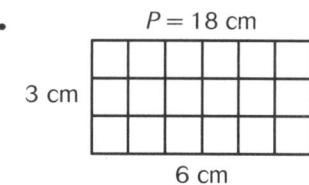

3. $P = 22$ m
4 m × 7 m

_____ _____ _____
_____ _____ _____

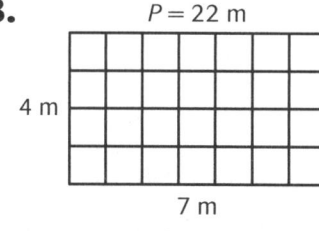

© Pearson Education, Inc.

61

Name _____

Math Diagnosis and Intervention System

Intervention Lesson **K31**

Rectangles with the Same Area (continued)

Draw a rectangle with the same area as the one shown. Then find the perimeter of each.

4. $P = 14$ ft; 3 ft by 4 ft

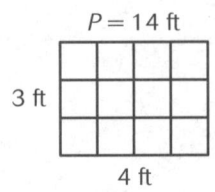

5. $P = 24$ yd; 2 yd by 10 yd

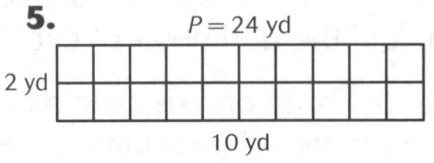

6. $P = 20$ mm; 4 mm by 6 mm

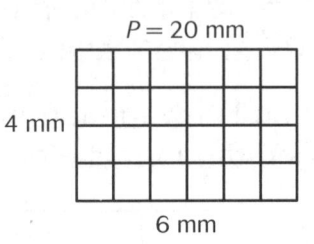

Draw a rectangle with the same perimeter as the one shown. Then find the area of each.

7. $A = 4\ \text{in.}^2$; 2 in. by 2 in.

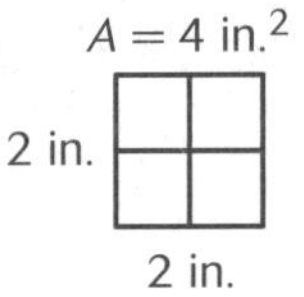

8. $A = 15\ \text{cm}^2$; 3 cm by 5 cm

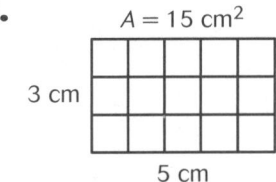

9. $A = 20\ \text{yd}^2$; 4 yd by 5 yd

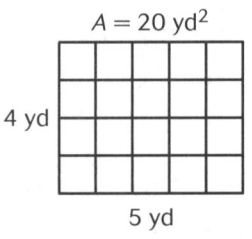

Test Prep Circle the correct letter for the answer.

10. Which are the dimensions of a rectangle with the same area as the one at the right?

    $P = 22$ cm; 5 cm by 6 cm

    A 11 cm by 2 cm

    B 30 cm by 2 cm

    C 22 cm by 1 cm

    D 10 cm by 3 cm

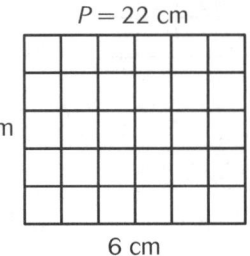

62

Name _____

Intervention Lesson **K32**

Area of a Circle

Example 1

Find the area of a circle with a radius of 14 millimeters.

$A = \pi r^2$

$A = \pi \times 14^2$

$A \approx \frac{22}{7} \times \frac{196}{1} = \frac{4{,}312}{7} = 616$

The area of the circle is about 616 square millimeters.

Example 2

Find the area of a circle with a diameter of 20 feet. Remember, if $d = 20$, $r = 10$.

$A = \pi r^2$

$A = \pi \times 10^2$

$A \approx 3.14 \times 100$

$A \approx 314$

The area of the circle is about 314 square feet.

Find the area of each circle to the nearest whole number. Use either 3.14 or $\frac{22}{7}$ for π.

1. 28 yd

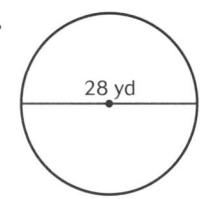

2. 12 m

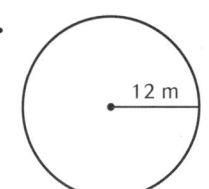

3. 16 cm

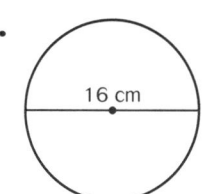

4. 2 in.

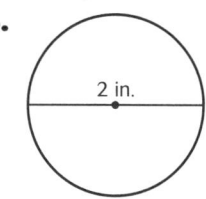

5. 14 ft

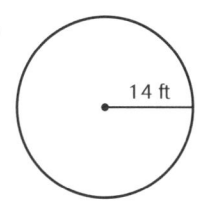

6. 15 ft

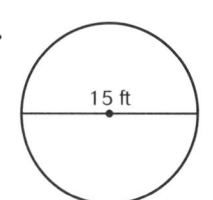

7. 13 mm

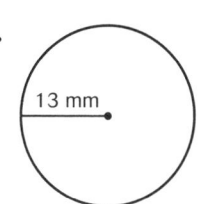

8. 35 m

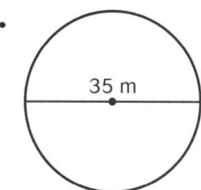

9. 9.7 ft

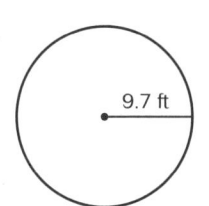

10. 3.6 cm

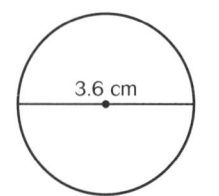

11. 5.7 yd

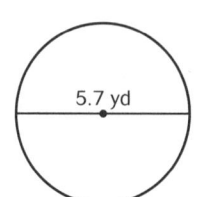

12. 8.7 mm

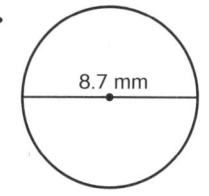

63

Name _____

Intervention Lesson **K32**

Area of a Circle (continued)

Find the area of each circle to the nearest whole number. Use either 3.14 or $\frac{22}{7}$ for π.

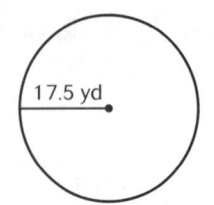

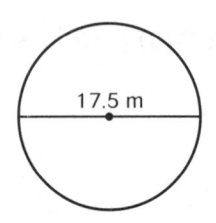

13. (circle, 12.3 m)

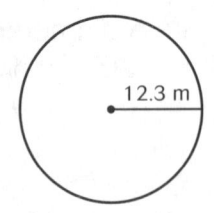

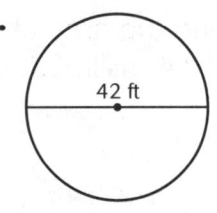

14. (circle, 17.5 yd)

15. (circle, 17.5 m)

16. (circle, 42 ft)

17. (circle, 9.6 m)

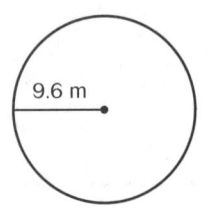

18. (circle, 100 mm)

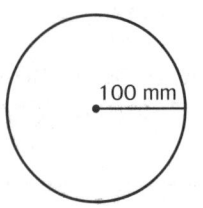

19. (circle, 13.7 in.)

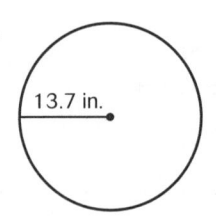

20. (circle, 4.9 cm)

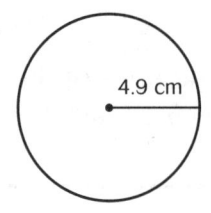

21. $d = 19.5$ m

22. $r = 7.6$ ft

23. $r = 6.9$ cm

24. $d = 18$ in.

25. $r = 0.6$ cm

26. $d = 22.4$ yd

27. $d = 4$ mm

28. $r = 7.1$ ft

29. Find the area of a circle to the nearest whole number if the diameter is 43 meters.

30. **Math Reasoning** Chase used 3.14 for π and found the circumference of a circle to be 47.1 feet. Find the area of the circle to the nearest whole number.

Test Prep Circle the correct letter for the answer.

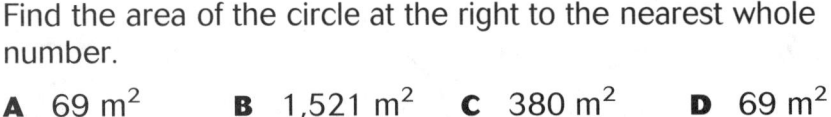

31. Find the area of the circle at the right to the nearest whole number.

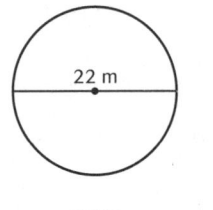

    A 69 m²   **B** 1,521 m²   **C** 380 m²   **D** 69 m²

    (circle, 22 m)

32. Find the area of the circle at the right to the nearest whole number.

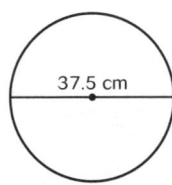

    A 118 cm²   **B** 4,418 cm²   **C** 59 cm²   **D** 1,104 cm²

    (circle, 37.5 cm)

Name _____

Intervention Lesson **K33**

Surface Area

Example

A figure having the dimensions shown at the left below could be cut out and folded to form the rectangular prism shown at the right. What is the surface area of the rectangular prism?

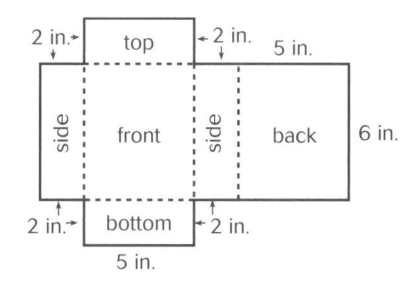

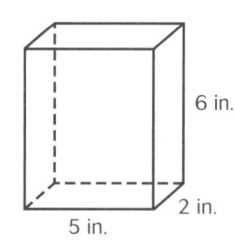

Add the areas of all the faces to find the surface area.

$$\text{Surface area} = \underset{\text{front}}{(5 \times 6)} + \underset{\text{back}}{(5 \times 6)} + \underset{\text{side}}{(2 \times 6)} + \underset{\text{side}}{(2 \times 6)} + \underset{\text{top}}{(5 \times 2)} + \underset{\text{bottom}}{(5 \times 2)}$$

$$= 30 + 30 + 12 + 12 + 10 + 10$$

$$= 104 \text{ in.}^2$$

Find the surface area of each figure.

1. 3 in., 4 in., 10 in.

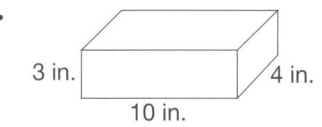

2. 9 ft, 2 ft, 3 ft

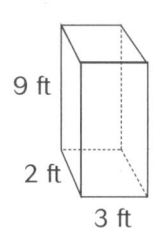

3. 5 in., 6 in., 4 in.

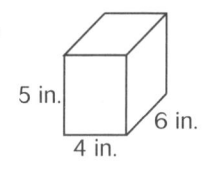

4. 3 yd, 2 yd, 2 yd

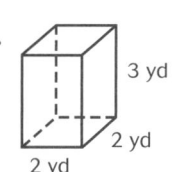

5. 4 in., 3 in., 8 in.

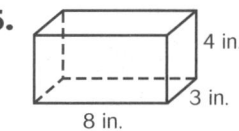

6. 5 m, 12 m, 15 m

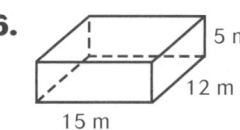

Surface Area (continued)

Find the surface area of each figure.

7. 7 cm, 4 cm, 4 cm

_____

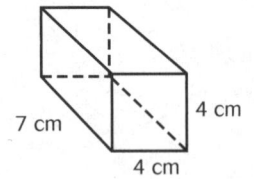

8. 10 in., 5 in., 6 in.

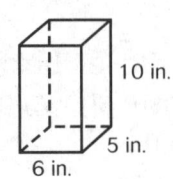

_____

9. 6 m, 7 m, 7 m

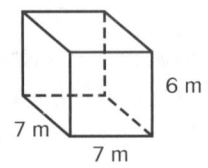

_____

10. 12 in., 14 in., 20 in.

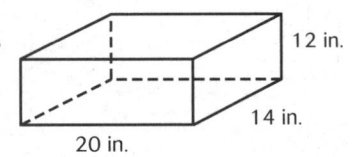

_____

11. 12 in., 12 in., 24 in.

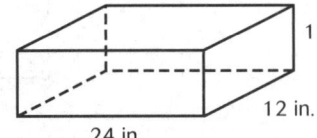

_____

12. 8 m, 8 m, 8 m

_____

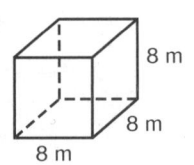

13. Mental Math Find the surface area of a cube with 100 centimeter edges.

_____

14. What is the surface area of a rectangular prism that is 9 yards wide, 10 yards long, and 11 yards high?

_____

Test Prep Circle the correct letter for the answer.

15. Find the surface area of the rectangular prism.

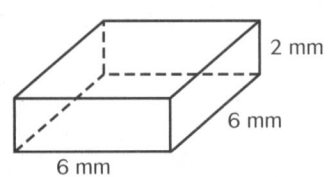

2 mm, 6 mm, 6 mm

    A 100 mm²   **C** 80 mm²

    B 60 mm²   **D** 120 mm²

16. What is the surface area of a rectangular prism that is 5 feet wide, 6 feet long, and 7 feet high?

    A 214 ft²   **C** 107 ft²

    B 210 ft²   **D** 179 ft²

Name _____

Intervention Lesson **K34**

Comparing Volume and Surface Area

Example 1

Volume is the number of cubic units needed to fill the space in the figure.

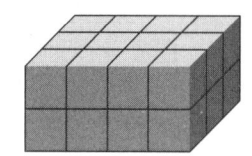

Find the volume of the figure at the right.

The bottom row is 4 cubes long and 3 cubes wide, so
$l \times w = 4 \times 3 = 12$ square units.

The figure is 2 cubes high, so $12 \times 2 = 24$ cubic units.

Example 2

The surface area of a figure is the sum of all the areas of its faces.

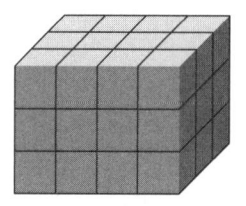

Find the surface area of the figure at the right.

2(area of front face) + 2(area of top face) + 2(area of right face)

$2(4 \times 3) + 2(4 \times 3) + 2(3 \times 3)$

$2(12) + 2(12) + 2(9)$

$24 + 24 + 18 = 66$ square units

Find the surface area and volume of each figure.

1.

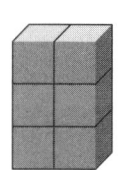

_____

2.

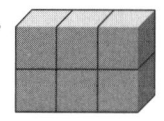

_____

3.

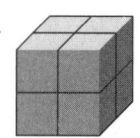

_____

4.

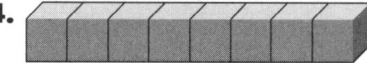

_____

67

Name _____

Intervention Lesson **K34**

Comparing Volume and Surface Area (continued)

Find the surface area and volume of each figure.

5.

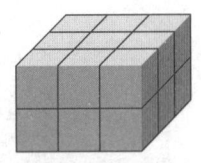

6.

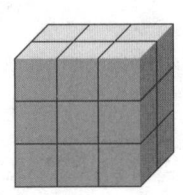

7.

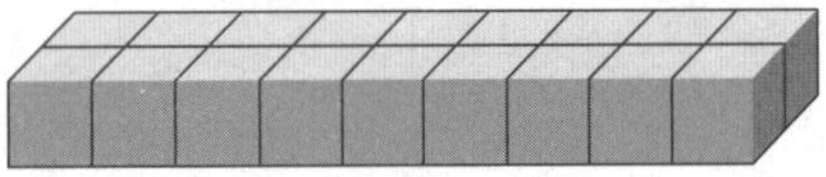

8.

9. Janet needs to determine how much wrapping paper she needs to wrap three presents of the same size. Will she need to determine the surface area or volume of the presents? Explain.

_____

Test Prep Circle the correct letter for the answer.

10. Which is the surface area of the figure?

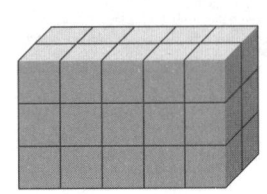

   A 15 square units   C 30 square units
   B 31 square units   D 62 square units

68

Name _____

Intervention Lesson **K35**

Volume

Example

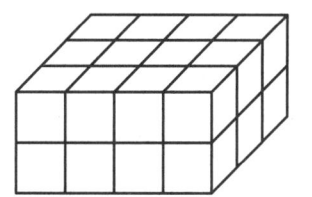

Find the volume of the figure.

The *volume* is the number of cubic units needed to fill the space in the figure.

You can see that the front row has 8 cubes, and there are 3 of these rows. The number of cubes is
8 + 8 + 8 = 24 cubes. So, the volume of the figure is 24 cubic units.

Find the volume of the figure.

1.

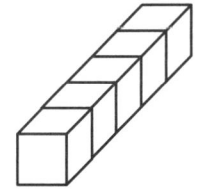

2.

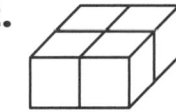

3.

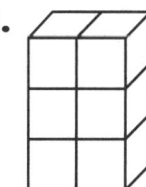

4.

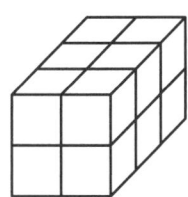

5.

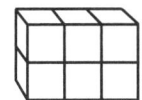

6.

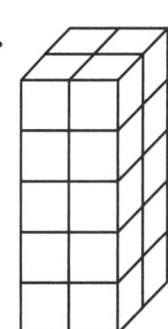

69

Name _____

Math Diagnosis and Intervention System

Intervention Lesson **K35**

Volume (continued)

Find the volume of the figure.

7.

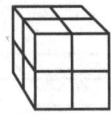

8.

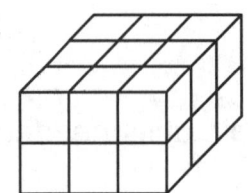

9.

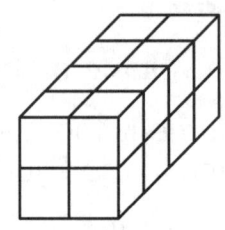

_____   _____   _____

10.

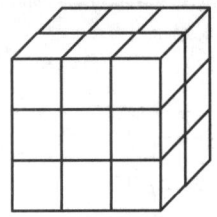

11.

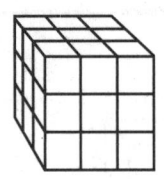

12.

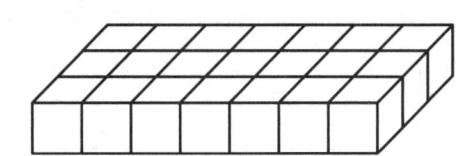

_____   _____   _____

13. **Writing in Math** Which of the boxes below will hold a larger volume? Explain.

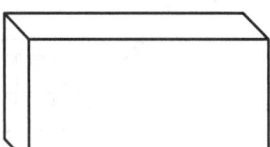

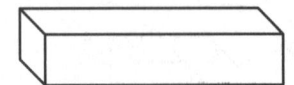

_____
_____
_____

Test Prep Circle the correct letter for the answer.

14. What is the volume of this figure? 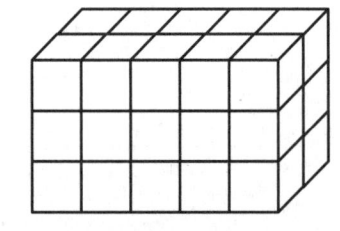
   - **A** 15 cubic units
   - **B** 20 cubic units
   - **C** 30 cubic units
   - **D** 45 cubic units

70

Name _____

Intervention Lesson **K36**

Volume

Example

Find the volume of the rectangular prism.

Use the formula

$V = l \times w \times h$

$V = 4 \times 7 \times 3$

$V = 84$ yd^3

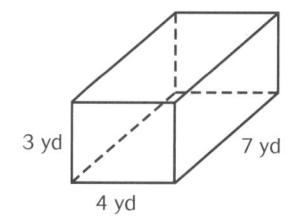

The volume of the rectangular prism is 84 yd^3.

Find the volume of each rectangular prism.

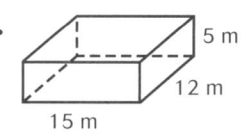

1. 3 m × 3 m × 3 m

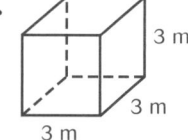

2. 8 in. × 3 in. × 4 in.

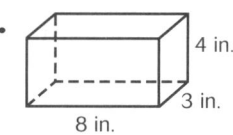

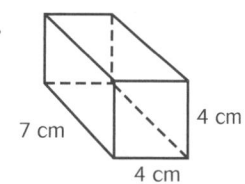

3. 7 cm × 4 cm × 4 cm

4. 2 yd × 2 yd × 3 yd

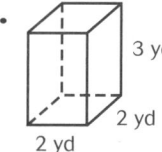

5. 10 ft × 10 ft × 10 ft

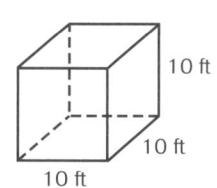

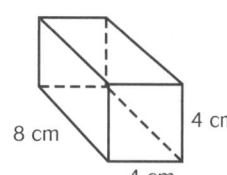

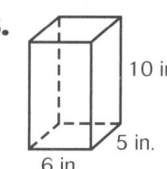

6. 15 m × 12 m × 5 m

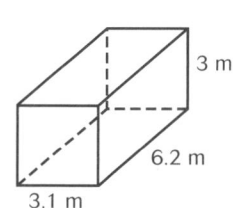

7. 8 cm × 4 cm × 4 cm

8. 6 in. × 5 in. × 10 in.

9. 3.1 m × 6.2 m × 3 m

10. 2.9 km × 2.9 km × 2.9 km

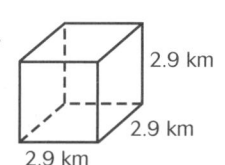

11. 4.5 yd × 1.5 yd × 1 yd

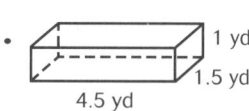

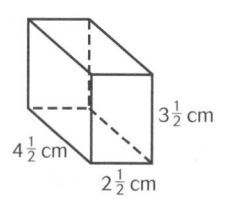

12. $4\frac{1}{2}$ cm × $2\frac{1}{2}$ cm × $3\frac{1}{2}$ cm

71

Name _____

Math Diagnosis and Intervention System

Intervention Lesson **K36**

Volume (continued)

Find each missing measurement.

13. $l = 14$ in.
    $w = 14$ in.
    $h = 7$ in.
    $V = \blacksquare$

    _____

14. $l = 3.1$ km
    $w = 5.2$ km
    $h = 4.4$ km
    $V = \blacksquare$

    _____

15. $l = 9.3$ ft
    $w = 2.4$ ft
    $h = 5.5$ ft
    $V = \blacksquare$

    _____

16. $l = 1\frac{1}{2}$ cm
    $w = 4\frac{1}{2}$ cm
    $h = 1\frac{1}{2}$ cm
    $V = \blacksquare$

    _____

17. $l = \blacksquare$
    $w = 2$ yd
    $h = 17$ yd
    $V = 510$ yd^3

    _____

18. $l = 2.1$ m
    $w = \blacksquare$
    $h = 5.4$ m
    $V = 74.844$ m^3

    _____

19. $l = 5.5$ in.
    $w = \blacksquare$
    $h = 4.3$ in.
    $V = 80.41$ in.^{3}

    _____

20. $l = 7$ mm
    $w = 5$ mm
    $h = \blacksquare$
    $V = 455$ mm^3

    _____

21. **Math Reasoning** How many cubic inches are in a cubic foot? _____

22. **Mental Math** Find the volume of a storage unit 10 feet wide, 4 feet long, and 4 feet high. _____

23. What is the volume of the storage unit in Exercise 22 in cubic yards to the nearest whole number? _____

Test Prep Circle the correct letter for the answer.

24. Find the volume of the rectangular prism at the right.
    - **A** 15.5 m^3
    - **B** 18.3 m^3
    - **C** 140.04 m^3
    - **D** 131.76 m^3

    4 m, 5.4 m, 6.1 m

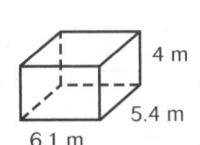

25. A rectangular prism has a volume of 69.3 ft^3. Its length is 3.5 feet and its width is 9 feet. What is its height?
    - **A** 19.8 ft
    - **B** 23.1 ft
    - **C** 2.2 ft
    - **D** 3.1 ft

Name _____

Intervention Lesson **K37**

Math Diagnosis and Intervention System

Volume of Triangular Prisms and Cylinders

Example 1

Find the volume of the triangular prism at the right.

Step 1 Find B, the area of the base.

$B = \frac{1}{2} b \times h$

$B = \frac{1}{2} \times 6 \times 4$

$B = 12$

Step 2 Use the volume formula.

$V = B \times h$

$V = 12 \times 5$

$V = 60$

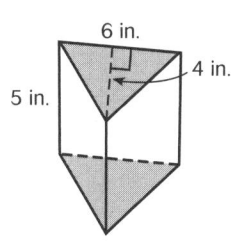

The volume of the triangular prism is 60 in.^{3}.

Example 2

Find the volume of the cylinder at the right.

Step 1 Find B, the area of the base.

$B = \pi r^2 = \pi \times 3^2$

$B \approx 3.14 \times 9$

$B \approx 28.26$

Step 2 Use the volume formula.

$V = B \times h$

$V \approx 28.26 \times 7.5$

$V \approx 211.95$

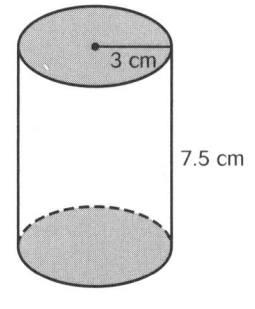

The volume of the cylinder is about 211.95 cm^3.

Find the volume for each space figure. Use either 3.14 or $\frac{22}{7}$ for π.

1. 4 ft, 7.2 ft, 3.5 ft

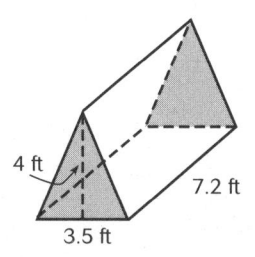

2. 3 m, 5.6 m

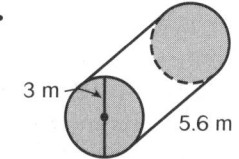

3. 5 yd, 3 yd, 7 yd

_____   _____   _____

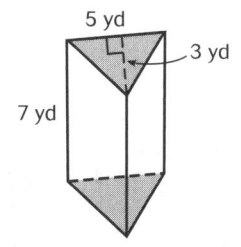

© Pearson Education, Inc.

73

Name _____

Math Diagnosis and Intervention System

Intervention Lesson **K37**

Volume of Triangular Prisms and Cylinders (continued)

Find the volume for each space figure. Use either 3.14 or $\frac{22}{7}$ for π.

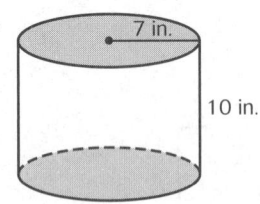

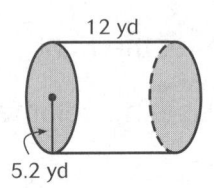

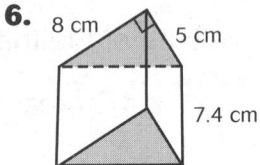

4. 7 in., 10 in. (cylinder)

5. 12 yd, 5.2 yd (cylinder)

6. 8 cm, 5 cm, 7.4 cm (triangular prism)

_____   _____   _____

Carlos is making candles using molds shown at the right.

7. If wax costs 3¢ per square inch, how much will the wax cost to make a cylinder-shaped candle? Use 3.14 for π.

(cylinder: 4 in., 6 in.)

_____

8. How much will the wax cost to make a triangular prism candle?

(triangular prism: 5 in., 2 in., 7 in.)

_____

9. If Carlos sells each candle for the same price, which candle yields more profit?

_____

10. Number Sense If the diameter and height are doubled for a cylinder, how many times larger is the new volume?

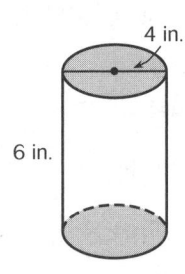

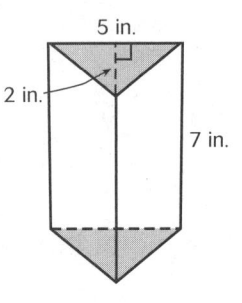

_____

Test Prep Circle the correct letter for the answer.

11. A cylinder has a diameter of 3.1 inches and a height of 7 inches. Find the volume rounded to the nearest tenth.

   A 52.8 in.^{3} **B** 21.7 in.^{3} **C** 67.3 in.^{3} **D** 21.1 in.^{3}

12. Find the volume of the figure at the right.

   A 90 m^3 **B** 15 m^3 **C** 45 m^3 **D** 30 m^3

(triangular prism: 4 m, 3 m, 7.5 m)

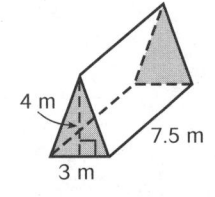

Name _____

Intervention Lesson **K38**

Solid Figures

Example 1

Objects that have length, width, and height are called **solid figures.** Name each of the following solid figures.

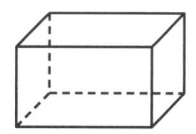

Rectangular prism 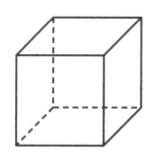   Cube    Pyramid 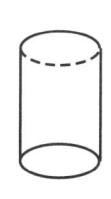   Cylinder    Cone 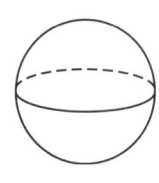   Sphere

Example 2

Objects that do not roll have faces. Where 2 faces meet is an edge. Where 2 or more edges meet is a corner.

The pyramid has 1 face shaped like a square and 4 faces shaped like triangles. It has 8 edges and 5 corners.

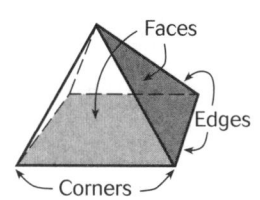

Name each solid figure.

1. _____

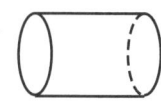

2. _____

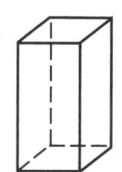

3. _____

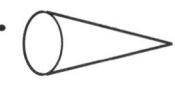

4. Which solid figure has 2 flat surfaces that are circles?

_____

Name _____

Math Diagnosis and Intervention System

Intervention Lesson **K38**

Solid Figures (continued)

Name each solid figure.

5. _____ 
6. _____ 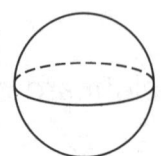
7. _____

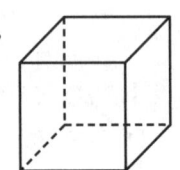

Name the solid figure that each object looks like.

8. _____ 
9. _____ 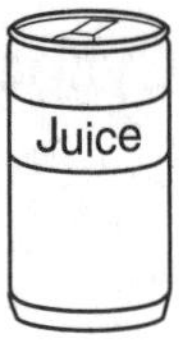
10. _____

Use the figures on the previous page to answer Questions 11–14.

11. Which of the 6 solid figures has no corners?

_____

12. Which of the 6 solid figures has 6 rectangular faces?

_____

13. How many edges does the cube have?

_____

14. Which 3 figures have no corners?

_____

Test Prep Circle the correct letter for the answer.

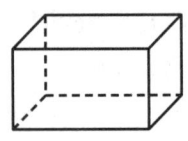

15. What is the name of this figure?

   A Cube   **C** Pyramid
   B Rectangular prism   **D** Cylinder

76

Lines, Segments, Rays, and Angles

Example

Write *right angle*, *acute angle*, or *obtuse angle* to name each angle.

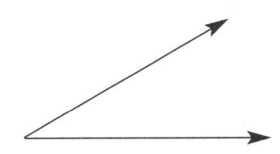

This is an acute angle since it is smaller than a right angle.

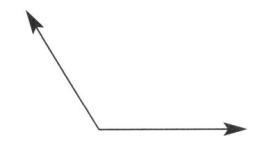

This is an obtuse angle since it is larger than a right angle.

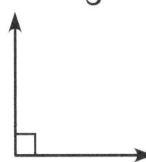

This is a right angle since it is exactly 90°.

Write *right angle*, *acute angle*, or *obtuse angle* to name each angle.

1. _____

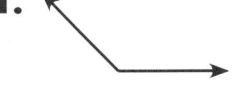

2. _____

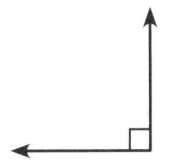

3. _____

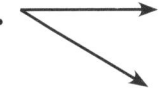

What kind of angle do the hands of each clock show?

4. _____

5. _____

6. _____

Name _____

Intervention Lesson **K39**

Math Diagnosis and Intervention System

Lines, Segments, Rays, and Angles (continued)

Write *right angle, acute angle*, or *obtuse angle* to name each angle.

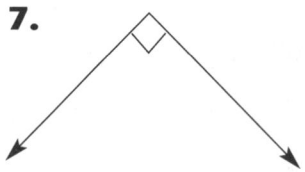

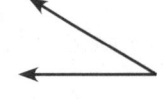

7. _____ 8. _____ 9. _____

What kind of angle do the hands of each clock show?

10. _____ 11. _____ 12. _____

13. Look at the angle formed by the number 7. What kind of angle does it form?

_____

Test Prep Circle the correct letter for the answer.

14. Classify this angle.

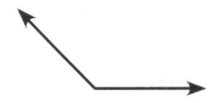

A Obtuse **B** Acute **C** Right **D** Straight

78

Name _____

Intervention Lesson **K40**

Math Diagnosis and Intervention System

Plane Figures

Example 1

Name the figure to the right.

The figure has 6 sides and 6 corners, so it is a hexagon.

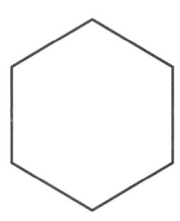

Example 2

What do the following figures have in common?

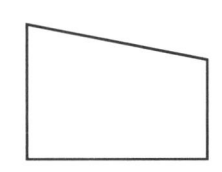

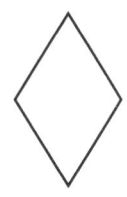

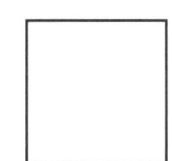

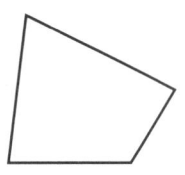

Each of the figures has 4 sides and 4 corners, so they are all quadrilaterals.

Name each figure. Then tell the number of sides and the number of corners each figure has.

1. _____

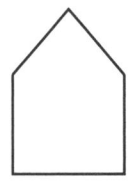

2. _____

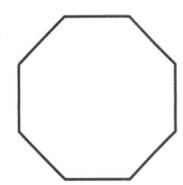

3. _____

4. _____

79

Name _____

Math Diagnosis and Intervention System

Intervention Lesson **K40**

Plane Figures (continued)

Name each plane figure. Then tell the number of sides and the number of corners each figure has.

5. _____

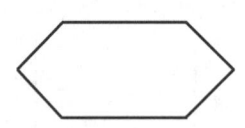

6. _____

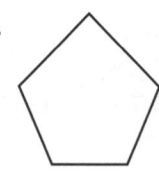

7. _____

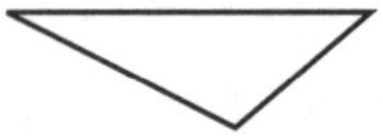

8. _____

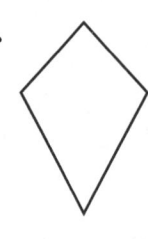

9. _____

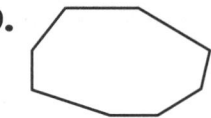

10. _____

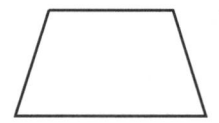

11. What is the shape of the cover of your math textbook?

   _____

12. **Reasoning** Is any plane figure with three sides and three corners a triangle?

   _____

Test Prep Circle the correct letter for the answer.

13. Which is true?

   A A hexagon has 5 sides.

   B An octagon has 8 corners.

   C A triangle has 2 corners.

   D A quadrilateral has 6 sides.

80

Intervention Lesson **K41**

Classifying Triangles Using Sides and Angles

Example 1
Describe triangles by their sides.

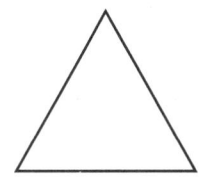

This is an **equilateral triangle**. All sides are the same length.

This is an **isosceles triangle**. At least two sides are the same length.

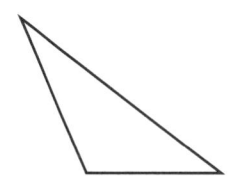

This is a **scalene triangle**. No sides are the same length.

Example 2
Name the triangles by the kinds of angles they have.

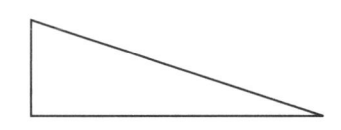

This is a **right triangle**. It has exactly one right angle.

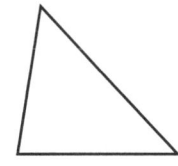

This is an **acute triangle**. It has 3 acute angles.

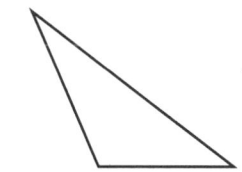

This is an **obtuse triangle**. It has exactly one obtuse angle.

Tell if each triangle is equilateral, isosceles, or scalene.

1. _____

2. _____

3. _____

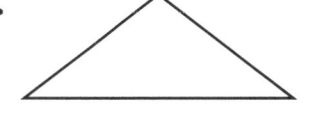

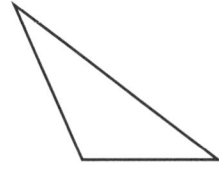

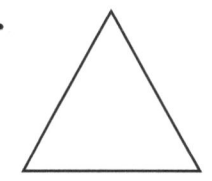

Tell the number of sides that are the same length for each triangle.

4. scalene _____

5. equilateral _____

6. isosceles _____

Triangles (continued)

Tell if each triangle is right, acute, or obtuse.

7.

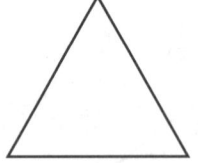

8.

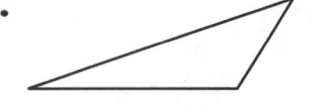

9.

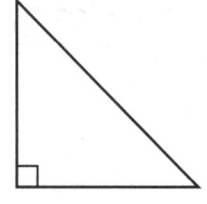

_____   _____   _____

10. How many acute angles does an acute triangle have? _____

11. How many obtuse angles does an obtuse triangle have? _____

12. How many right angles does a right triangle have? _____

13. **Reasoning** How many acute angles does a right triangle have? _____

14. Describe this triangle by its sides and by its angles. (Hint: Give it two names.)

    _____   _____

Test Prep Circle the correct letter for the answer.

15. Which term describes this triangle?

    A Acute   **B** Right   **C** Equilateral   **D** Obtuse

16. How many sides of an isosceles triangle are the same length?

    A One   **B** Two   **C** Three   **D** None

Name _____

Intervention Lesson **K42**

Quadrilaterals

Example

Name the quadrilaterals.

A **parallelogram** has two pairs of parallel sides and opposite sides which are the same length.

A **rhombus** has two pairs of parallel sides and all sides are the same length.

A **rectangle** has two pairs of parallel sides, opposite sides which are the same length, and 4 right angles.

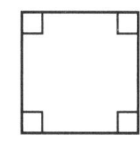

A **square** has two pairs of parallel sides, all sides the same length, and 4 right angles.

Write the name of each quadrilateral.

1. _____ 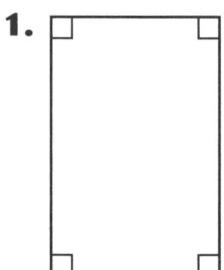
2. _____ 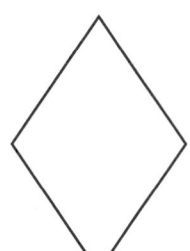
3. _____

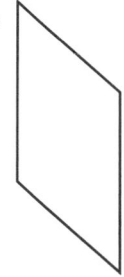

83

Name _____

Math Diagnosis and Intervention System
Intervention Lesson **K42**

Quadrilaterals (continued)

Write the name of each quadrilateral.

4. _____

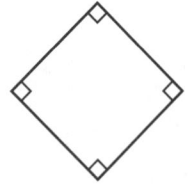

5. _____

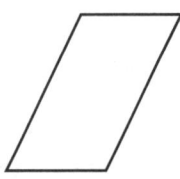

6. _____

7. I have two pairs of parallel sides, and all of my sides are equal, but I have no right angles. What quadrilateral am I? _____

8. I have two pairs of parallel sides and 4 right angles, but all 4 of my sides are not equal. What quadrilateral am I? _____

9. Name all of the quadrilaterals in the picture at the right.

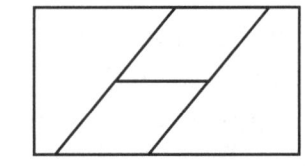

_____

10. **Writing in Math** Can a quadrilateral be both a rhombus and a parallelogram? Explain your answer.

_____

_____

_____

Test Prep Circle the correct letter for the answer.

11. What is the name of this figure?

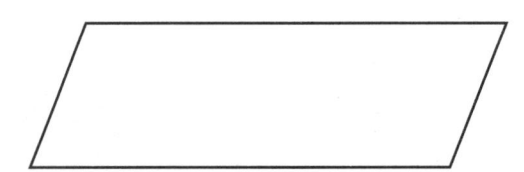

   A Parallelogram   **B** Square   **C** Rhombus   **D** Rectangle

84

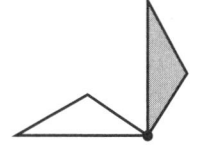

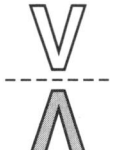

Name _____

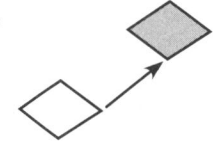

Intervention Lesson **K43**

Slides, Flips, and Turns

Example 1

Does the diagram at the right show a slide, flip, or turn?

Compare the position of the two figures. The shaded figure is a reflection of the unshaded figure across the dotted line.

So, the diagram shows a flip.

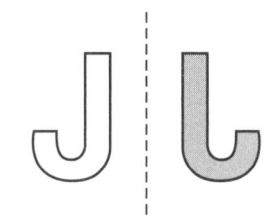

Example 2

Does the diagram at the right show a slide, flip, or turn?

The shaded figure has been turned around the point. So, the diagram shows a turn.

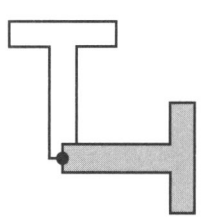

Write slide, flip, or turn for each diagram.

1.

2.

3.

4.

5.

6.

85

Name _____

Intervention Lesson K43

Slides, Flips, and Turns (continued)

Write slide, flip, or turn for each diagram.

7. _____

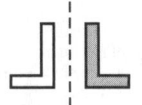

8. _____

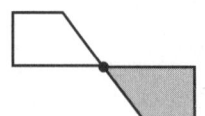

9. _____

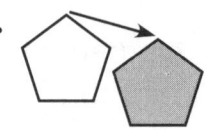

10. _____

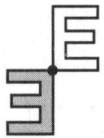

11. _____

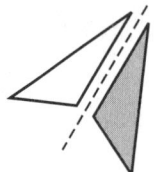

12. _____

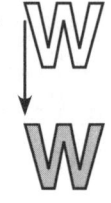

Use the figures to the right to answer Questions 13 and 14.

13. Are Figures 1 and 2 related by a slide, a flip, or a turn? _____

14. Are Figures 1 and 3 related by a slide, a flip, or a turn? _____

Figure 1
Figure 2
Figure 3

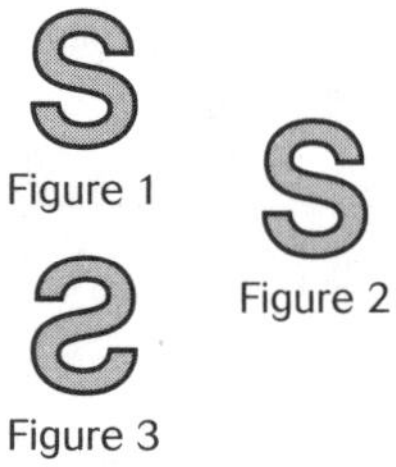

Test Prep Circle the correct letter for the answer.

15. Which describes how the figure at the right was moved from A to B?

   A Slide **C** Turn
   B Flip   **D** Flip then slide

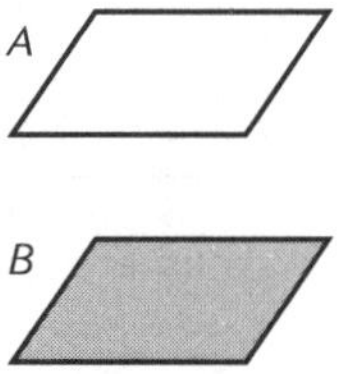

86

Name _____

Intervention Lesson **K44**

Line Symmetry

Example 1

Tell how many lines of symmetry each figure has.

a. 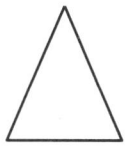 An isosceles triangle has 1 line of symmetry.

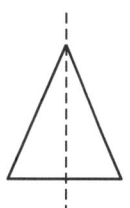

b.  A rhombus has 2 lines of symmetry.

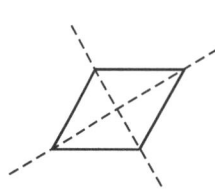

Example 2

Is the dashed line a line of symmetry for the figure below?

Imagine folding the figure along the dotted line. Since the two halves would not match exactly, the dashed line is not a line of symmetry.

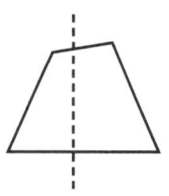

Is the dashed line a line of symmetry? Write *yes* or *no*.

1.

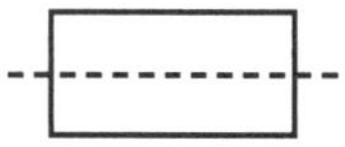

2.

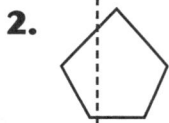

3.

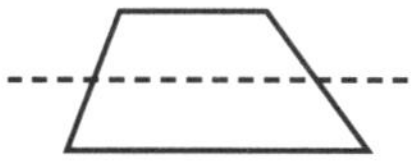

4.

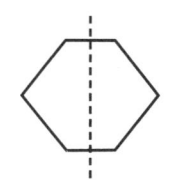

5.

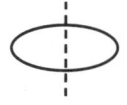

6.

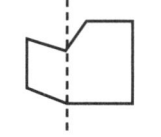

87

Name _____

Intervention Lesson K44

Math Diagnosis and Intervention System

Line Symmetry (continued)

Tell how many lines of symmetry the figure has.

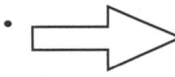

7. _____

8. _____

9. _____

10. _____

11. _____

12. _____

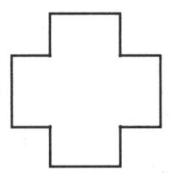

13. Draw all of the lines of symmetry on the figure at the right.

14. Draw all of the lines of symmetry on the hexagon at the right. Hint: There are six lines of symmetry.

Test Prep Choose the correct letter for the answer.

15. Which letter has more than one line of symmetry?

A. A B. S C. X D. D

88

Name _____

Intervention Lesson **K45**

Polygons

Example 1

What type of figure is shown at the right?

The figure is a polygon. It has 5 sides, so it is a pentagon.

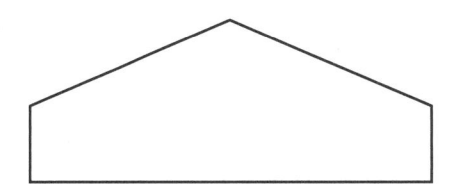

Example 2

Explain why these figures are not polygons.

a. 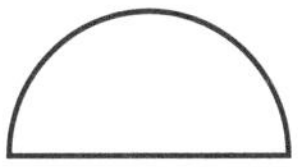 This figure is not a polygon because it is not made up of all line segments.

b.  This figure is not a polygon because the line segments do not intersect only at their endpoints.

c. 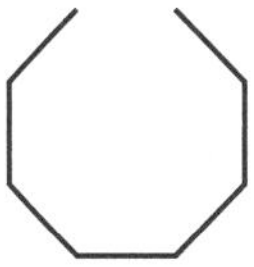 This figure is not a polygon because it is not closed.

Identify each polygon.

1. _____

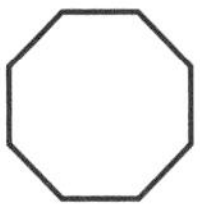

2. _____

3. _____

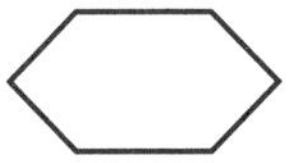

4. _____

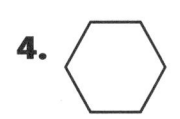

Tell if the figure is a polygon. Write *yes* or *no*.

5. E

6.

7.

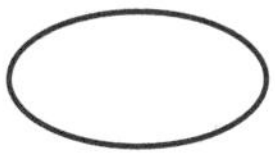

8. T

89

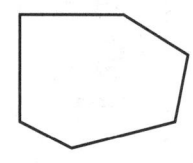

Name _____

Math Diagnosis and Intervention System
Intervention Lesson **K45**

Polygons (continued)

Tell if the figure is a polygon. Write *yes* or *no*. If it is a polygon, write its name.

9. D
_____

10.
_____

11.
_____

12.
_____

Explain why the figure is not a polygon.

13.
_____
_____
_____

14.
_____
_____
_____

15.
_____
_____
_____

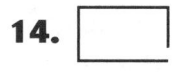

16. **Math Reasoning** What is the least number of sides a polygon can have? _____

17. **Math Reasoning** Can a polygon have more than 8 sides? Explain.
_____
_____

Test Prep Circle the correct letter for the answer.

18. What is the name of this figure?

    A Quadrilateral   **C** Hexagon

    B Pentagon   **D** Octagon

Name _____

Math Diagnosis and Intervention System

Intervention Lesson **K46**

Geometric Ideas

Example 1

Draw and label an example of a plane ABC.

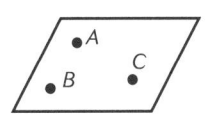

Example 2

Draw and label an example of $\overleftrightarrow{AB}$ intersects $\overleftrightarrow{LM}$.

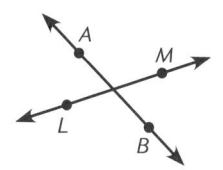

Draw and label an example of each.

1. ray GH

2. line segment RS

3. plane IJK

4. $\overleftrightarrow{TV}$ is parallel to $\overleftrightarrow{WX}$

5. $\overline{EF}$ is perpendicular to $\overline{JK}$

6. $\overrightarrow{YZ}$ intersects $\overrightarrow{AB}$

7. $\overline{CD}$ intersects $\overrightarrow{HJ}$

8. $\overleftrightarrow{LM}$ is perpendicular to $\overrightarrow{NP}$

9. point C

91

Name _____

Intervention Lesson **K46**

Math Diagnosis and Intervention System

Geometric Ideas (continued)

Draw and label an example of each.

10. two perpendicular lines   **11.** two parallel lines   **12.** plane *JKL*

13. ray *HJ*   **14.** line segment *KL*   **15.** line *RS*

Use the drawing at the right for Exercises 16 and 17.

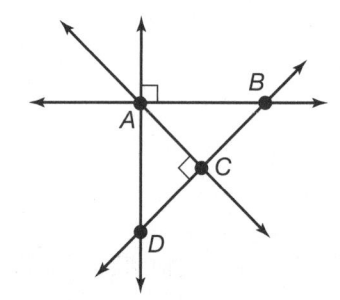

16. Name 3 line segments.   **17.** Name 2 lines.

_____   _____

_____   _____

18. Math Reasoning What geometric idea is suggested by a floor in a room? What geometric idea is suggested by the edge of a table?

_____

Test Prep Circle the correct letter for the answer.

19. Which of these describes point *F*?

   A It is the endpoint of $\overline{AD}$.

   B It is the endpoint of $\overline{FG}$.

   C It is on $\overline{AC}$.

   D It is on $\overline{AG}$.

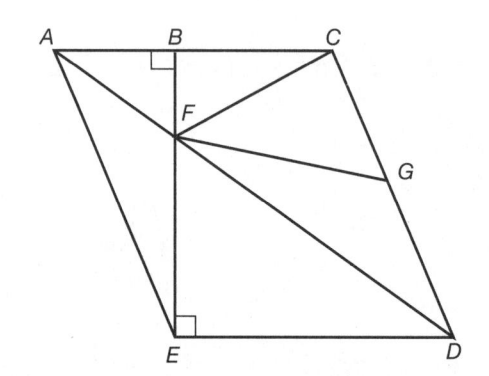

92

Name _____

Intervention Lesson **K47**

Circles

Example 1

Find the radius of the circle.

diameter: 24 m
radius: 24 m ÷ 2 = 12 m
↑
divide by 2

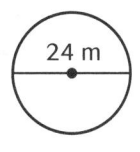

Example 2

Estimate the circumference of the circle in Example 1.

Multiply the diameter by 3.

3 × 24 m = 72 m

The circumference of the circle is about 72 meters.

Identify the part of each circle indicated by the arrow.

1.   _____

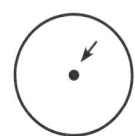

2.   _____

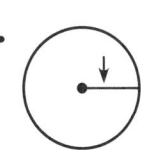

3.   _____

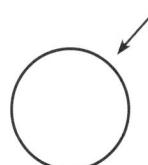

4.   _____

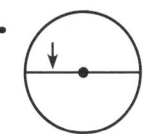

5. The diameter of a circle is 7 feet. Estimate its circumference.   _____

6. The radius of a circle is 11 centimeters. What is the diameter of the circle?   _____

93

Name _____

Math Diagnosis and Intervention System
Intervention Lesson **K47**

Circles (continued)

Find the radius or diameter of each circle. Estimate the circumference.

7. (circle with 6 in. diameter)

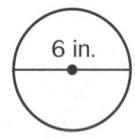

radius: _____

circumference: _____

8. (circle with 5 ft radius)

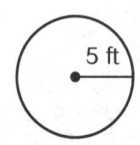

diameter: _____

circumference: _____

9. (circle with 18 cm diameter)

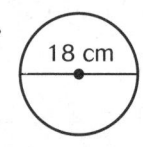

radius: _____

circumference: _____

10. The diameter of a circular flower bed is 10 feet. Estimate the circumference of the flower bed. _____

11. **Mental Math** The circumference of a circle is 24 meters. Estimate its diameter. _____

12. **Math Reasoning** Is it possible to draw a line segment with each endpoint on a circle, so that it is longer than the diameter of the circle? Explain.

_____

_____

Test Prep Circle the correct letter for the answer.

Use the circle at the right to answer Questions 13 and 14.

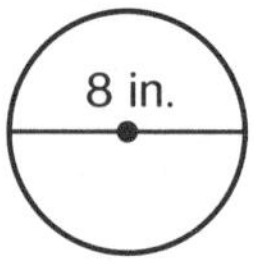

13. What is the length of the radius?

    A 2 inches   **B** 4 inches   **C** 8 inches   **D** 16 inches

(circle with 8 in. radius)

14. Estimate the circumference.

    A about 6 inches   **C** about 24 inches

    B about 12 inches.   **D** about 48 inches

94

Name _____

Intervention Lesson **K48**

Congruent and Similar Figures

Example 1

Two figures that have exactly the same size and shape are **congruent** figures. Figures A and B are congruent because the sides and angles of Figure A are equal to the sides and angles of Figure B.

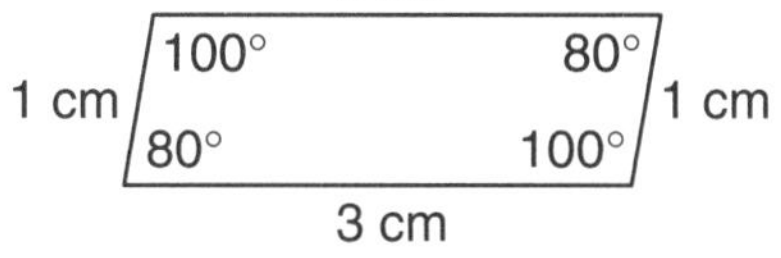

Figure A

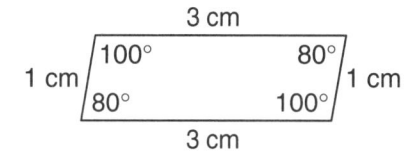

Figure B

Example 2

Similar figures have the same angle measures and the lengths of the sides in one figure can be multiplied by the same number to give the length of the sides in the other figure.

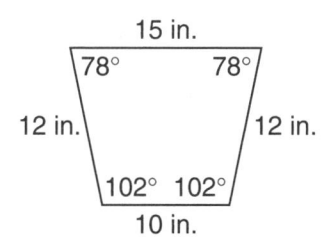

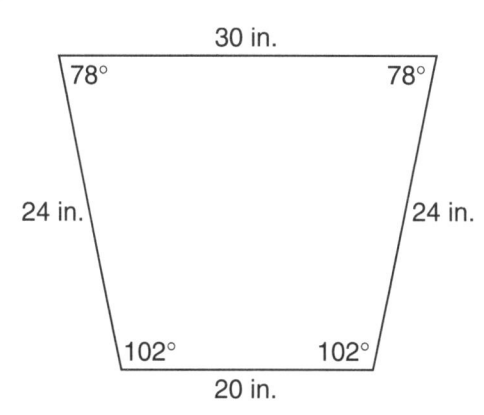

Tell if the two figures are congruent. Write *yes* or *no*.

1.

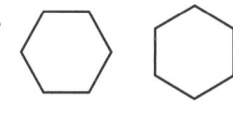

2.

3.

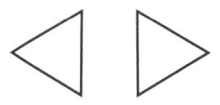

_____   _____   _____

4.

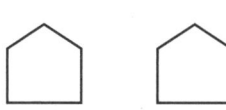

5.

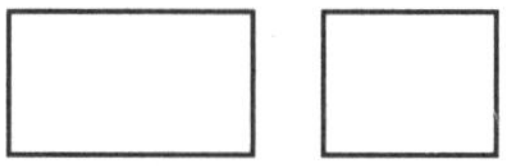

6.

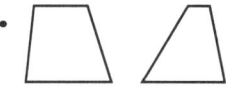

_____   _____   _____

95

Name _____

Math Diagnosis and Intervention System

Intervention Lesson **K48**

Congruent and Similar Figures (continued)

Tell if the two figures are similar. Write *yes* or *no*.

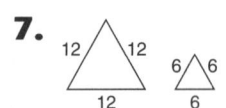

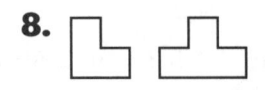

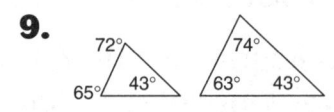

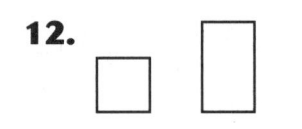

7. _____

8. _____

9. _____

10. _____

11. _____

12. _____

13. Divide the isosceles triangle shown at the right into 2 congruent right triangles.

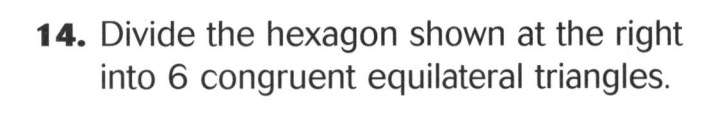

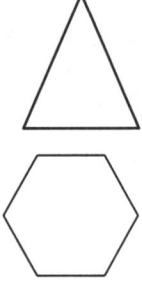

14. Divide the hexagon shown at the right into 6 congruent equilateral triangles.

15. Divide the rectangle shown at the right into 2 pairs of congruent triangles.

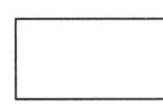

Test Prep Circle the correct letter for the answer.

16. Which figure is congruent to the one to the left?

A

B

C

D

96

Name _____

Intervention Lesson **K49**

Measuring and Classifying Angles

Use the following classifications to classify the angles.

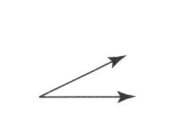

Acute angle
between 0° and 90°

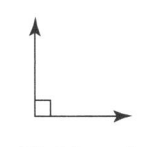

Right angle
exactly 90°

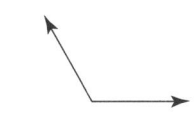

Obtuse angle
between 90° and 180°

Straight angle
exactly 180°

Example

Classify the angle as acute, right, or obtuse.
Then use a protractor to check the measure.

The angle looks more than 90°, so it is obtuse.
A protractor shows the measure to be 110°.

Classify each angle as acute, right, obtuse, or straight. Then measure the angle.

1.

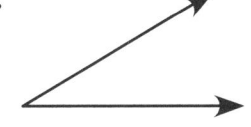

2.

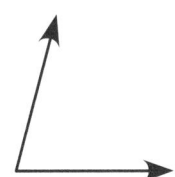

3.

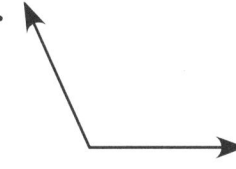

_____
_____

_____
_____

_____
_____

4.

5.

6.

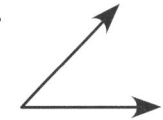

_____
_____

_____
_____

_____
_____

97

Name _____

Math Diagnosis and Intervention System
Intervention Lesson **K49**

Measuring and Classifying Angles (continued)

Classify each angle as acute, right, obtuse, or straight. Then measure the angle.

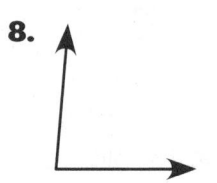

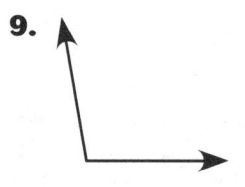

7.
8.
9.

_____ _____ _____
_____ _____ _____

Use a protractor to draw an angle with each measure.

10. 120°   **11.** 35°   **12.** 70°

13. Algebra A figure has four angles. The sum of its angles is 360°. Three of its angles measure 90°, 120°, and 70°. What kind of angle is the fourth angle?

_____

Test Prep Circle the correct letter for the answer.

14. Which is the measure of an obtuse angle?

  A 180°   **C** 90°
  B 100°   **D** 80°

15. Benjamin drew the angle at the right. How would you classify the angle? 157°

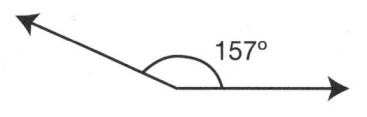

  A Straight
  B Obtuse
  C Right
  D Acute

98

Name _____

Math Diagnosis and Intervention System

Intervention Lesson **K50**

Triangles

Example

Describe each triangle below by both its sides and its angles.

a. 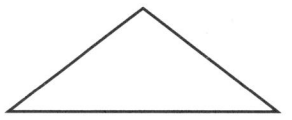 The triangle is both an obtuse triangle and an isosceles triangle.

b. 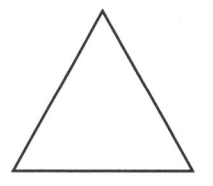 The triangle is both an acute triangle and an equilateral triangle.

c. 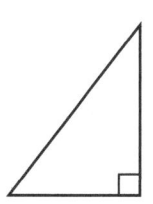 The triangle is both a right triangle and a scalene triangle.

Describe each triangle by its sides. Then describe it by its angles.

1. 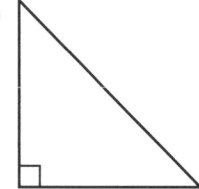
2. 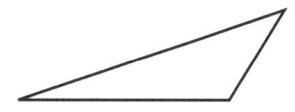
3.

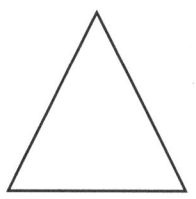

_____   _____   _____

_____   _____   _____

The lengths of the sides of a triangle are given. Describe each triangle by its sides.

4. 3 m, 3 m, 3 m   **5.** 2 ft, 4 ft, 3 ft   **6.** 6 in., 5 in., 6 in.

_____   _____   _____

99

Name _____

Math Diagnosis and Intervention System
Intervention Lesson **K50**

Triangles (continued)

Describe each triangle by its sides. Then describe it by its angles.

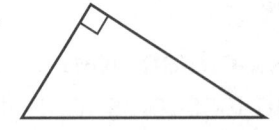

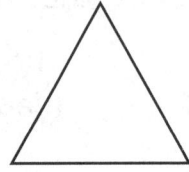

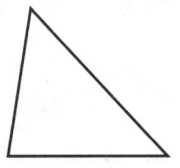

7. _____ 8. _____ 9. _____

The lengths of the sides of a triangle are given. Describe each triangle by its sides.

10. 12 cm, 12 cm, 10 cm   11. 6 in., 4 in., 3 in.   12. 5 ft, 5 ft, 5 ft

_____   _____   _____

Draw the figure described. If it is not possible, write so.

13. A right triangle that is also an equilateral triangle.

14. An acute triangle that is also a scalene triangle.

15. An obtuse triangle that is also an isosceles triangle.

Test Prep Circle the correct letter for the answer.

16. Name the kind of triangle.

    A Equilateral triangle   C Regular triangle
    B Isosceles triangle   D Scalene triangle

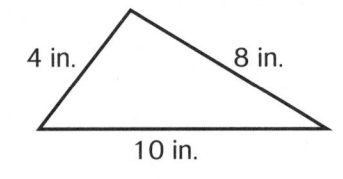

    4 in.   8 in.
    10 in.

100

Name _____

Intervention Lesson **K51**

Math Diagnosis and Intervention System

Quadrilaterals

Example

What type of quadrilateral is shown?

a.  This figure has all sides the same length and opposite sides are parallel, so it is a **rhombus**.

b.  This figure has both pairs of opposite sides parallel and 4 right angles, so it is a **rectangle**.

c. 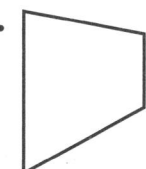 This figure has only one pair of parallel sides, so it is a **trapezoid**.

d. 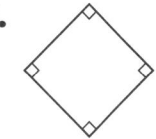 This figure has all sides the same length and 4 right angles, so it is a **square**.

e.  This figure has both pairs of opposite sides parallel, so it is a **parallelogram**.

What type of quadrilateral is shown?

1. _____

2. _____

3. _____

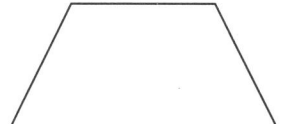

Name _____

Intervention Lesson **K51**

Quadrilaterals (continued)

What type of quadrilateral is shown?

4.

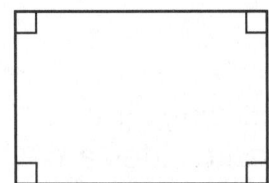

_____

5.

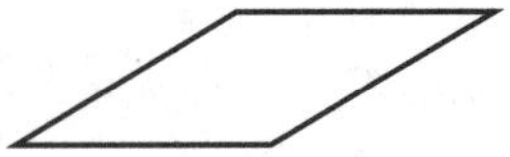

_____

6.

_____

7.

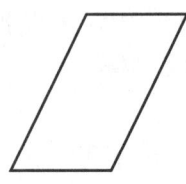

_____

8.

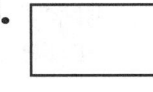

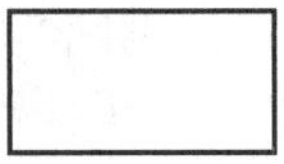

_____

9.

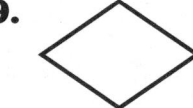

_____

10. Plot the set of ordered pairs (0, 0), (1, 4), (6, 0), (7, 4). Draw line segments to connect them in order. Then connect the last ordered pair to the first. Tell what type of quadrilateral is formed.

_____

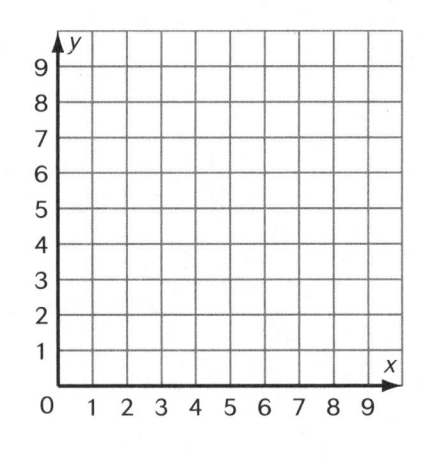

11. I am a parallelogram. I have 4 sides of equal length and no right angles. What am I?

_____

Test Prep Circle the correct letter for the answer.

12. Which is the name of this quadrilateral?

   A Parallelogram   **C** Rhombus
   B Trapezoid   **D** Rectangle

Name _____

Intervention Lesson **K52**

Transformations

Example 1

Transformations do not change the size or shape of a figure. There are 3 types of transformations.

A **slide,** or **translation,** moves a figure in a straight direction.

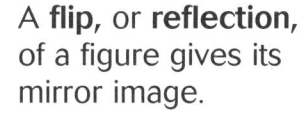

A **flip,** or **reflection,** of a figure gives its mirror image.

A **turn,** or **rotation,** moves a figure about a point.

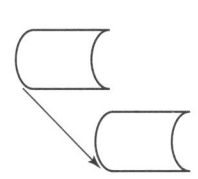

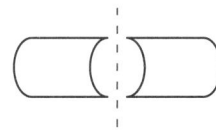

Example 2

Turns, or rotations, can also be measured in degrees. Here are some common turns. All of these turns are clockwise turns. Counterclockwise turns are in the opposite direction.

90° or $\frac{1}{4}$ turn   180° or $\frac{1}{2}$ turn   270° or $\frac{3}{4}$ turn   360° or full turn

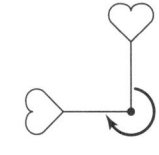

Tell whether the figures in each pair are related by a slide, a flip, or a turn. If a turn, describe it.

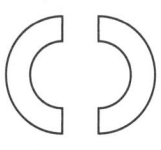

1.

2.

3.

_____   _____   _____

103

Intervention Lesson **K52**

Transformations (continued)

Tell whether the figures in each pair are related by a slide, a flip, or a turn. If a turn, describe it.

4. _____

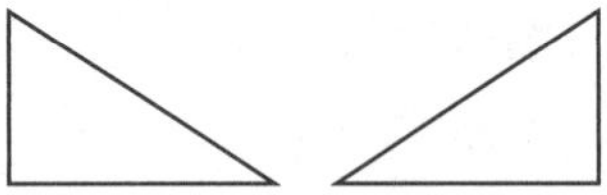

5. _____

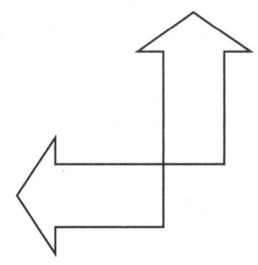

6. _____

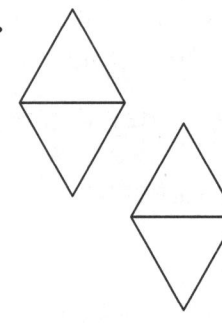

7. _____

8. _____

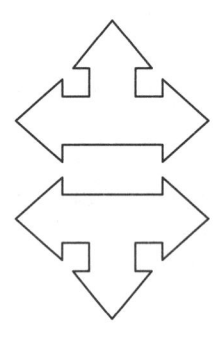

9. _____

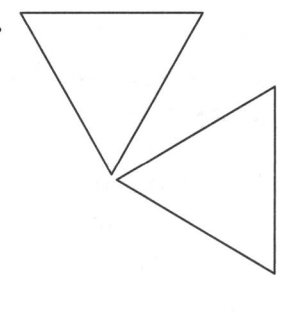

10. **Reasoning** Turning a figure to the right two times results in which single transformation?

_____

Test Prep Circle the correct letter for the answer.

11. Identify the transformation.

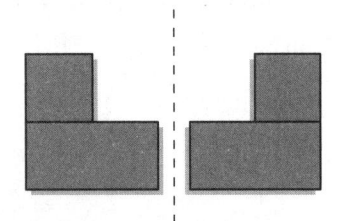

   A slide   C $\frac{1}{4}$ turn

   B flip   D $\frac{3}{4}$ turn

104

Name _____

Intervention Lesson **K53**

Solid Figures

Example

Name the solid figure and draw its base.

The solid has a triangle on bottom and comes to a point on top. Therefore it is a triangular pyramid.

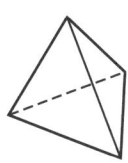

From the bottom you would see that the base is a triangle.

Name each solid figure and draw its base.

1.

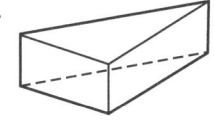

2.

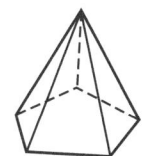

3.

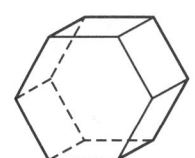

_____   _____   _____

4.

5.

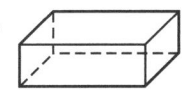

6.

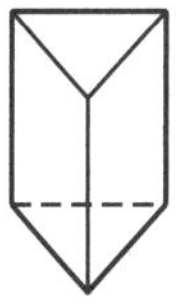

_____   _____   _____

105

Name _____

Intervention Lesson **K53**

Solid Figures (continued)

Name each solid figure and draw its base.

7.    8. 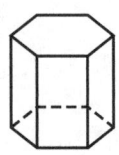   9.

_____   _____   _____

Draw the front, right, and top views of each three-dimensional object shown. There are no hidden cubes.

10. 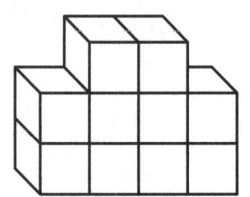   11. 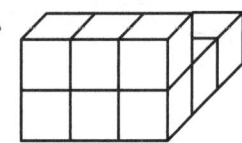   12.

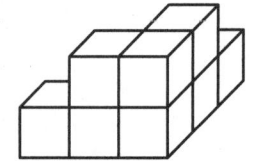

13. **Math Reasoning** Draw a pattern that can make the solid figure shown.

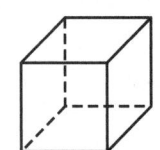

Test Prep Circle the correct letter for the answer.

14. Which shape is every side face of a prism?

    A Rectangle   **C** Triangle

    B Square   **D** Parallelogram

Name _____

Intervention Lesson **K54**

Views of Solid Figures

Example 1

A **net** is a plane figure that, when folded, creates a soild figure.

What solid figure will the net at the right form?

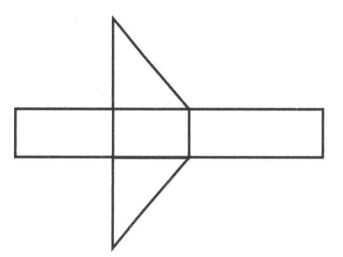

Think: What shapes make the net and what solid figure is made from those shapes?

The net is made of triangles and rectangles, so a triangular prism can be formed.

Example 2

You can show the top, front, and side views of a figure. This solid is made of unit cubes.

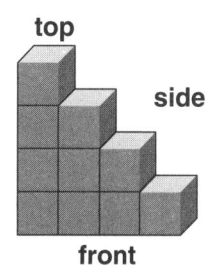

Top view—imagine looking straight down from up above.

Front view—imagine looking straight at the cubes.

Side view—imagine looking at the side.

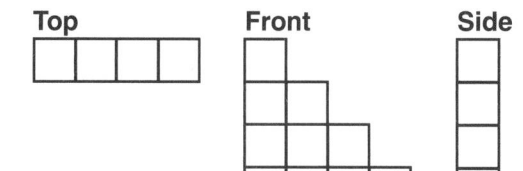

---

1. What solid does the net form?

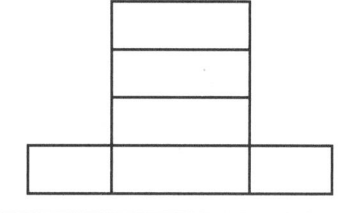

---

2. Draw front, side, and top views of the figure.

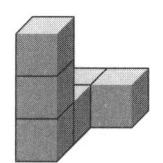

107

Name _____

Math Diagnosis and Intervention System
Intervention Lesson **K54**

Views of Solid Figures (continued)

What solid will each net form?

3.

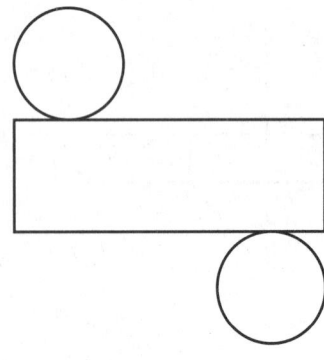

4.

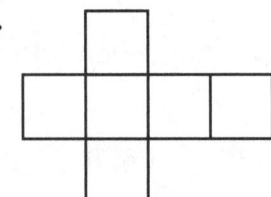

_____   _____

Draw front, side, and top views of each figure.

5.

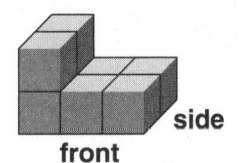

6.

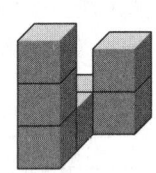

7. **Reasoning** Is the figure a net for a cube? Explain.

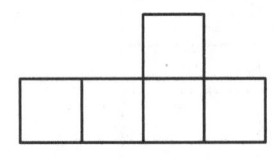

_____
_____

Test Prep Circle the correct letter for the answer.

8. Which net can be folded to make a cube?

A   B 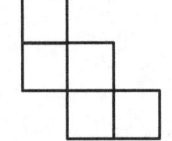   C 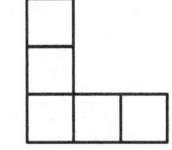   D

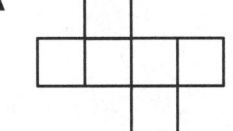

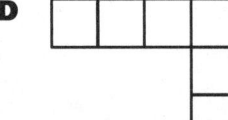

Name _____

Intervention Lesson **K55**

Angle Pairs

Example 1

Find the measure of ∠RPT in the figure at the right.

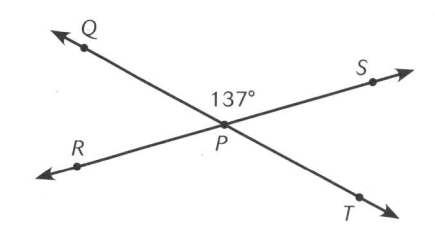

∠QPS and ∠RPT are vertical angles, so angles
m∠QPS = m∠RPT = 137°.

Example 2

Find the measure of ∠DBC in the figure at the right.

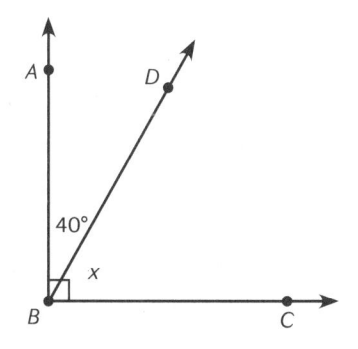

∠ABD and ∠DBC are adjacent, complementary angles
and m∠ABD = 40°. You can write and solve this equation
to find m∠DBC.

m∠ABD + m∠DBC = 90°
40 + x = 90
x = 50
m∠DBC = 50°

Find the measure of each angle labeled with a letter.

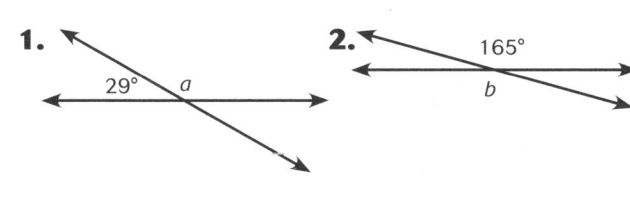

1. 29°, a

2. 165°, b

3. 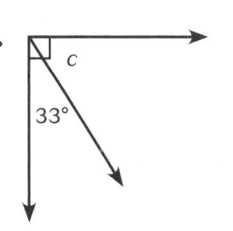 33°, c

4. 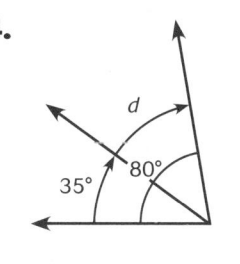 35°, 80°, d

_____ _____ _____ _____

Find the measure of an angle that is supplementary to an angle with each measure.

5. 26°   **6.** 135°   **7.** 90°   **8.** 32°

_____ _____ _____ _____

9. 172°   **10.** 4°   **11.** 80°   **12.** 166°

_____ _____ _____ _____

109

Name _____

Intervention Lesson **K55**

Angle Pairs (continued)

Find the measurement of an angle that is supplementary to an angle with each measure.

13. 55°   **14.** 96°   **15.** 7°   **16.** 178°

Find the measure of an angle that is complementary to an angle with each measure.

17. 84°   **18.** 4°   **19.** 16°   **20.** 72°

21. 32°   **22.** 50°   **23.** 17°   **24.** 9°

Find the measure of each angle at the right.

25. m∠NOT   **26.** m∠PON

27. m∠SOP

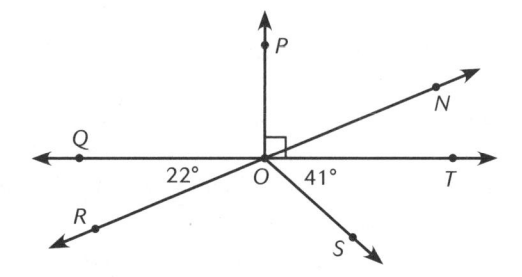

28. Math Reasoning Two angles are adjacent and complementary. One angle measure is twice as large as the other. Find the measure of the smaller angle. _____

Test Prep Circle the correct letter for the answer.

29. What is the measure of an angle complementary to a 48° angle?

     A 52°   **B** 132°   **C** 42°   **D** 142°

30. Find the measure of ∠KLM in the figure on the right.

     A 75°   **B** 80°   **C** 20°   **D** 160°

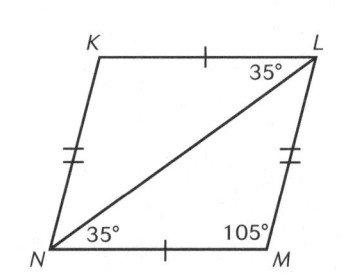

Name _____

Math Diagnosis and Intervention System

Intervention Lesson **K56**

Constructions

Example 1

Construct a segment congruent to $\overline{XY}$.

X •————————————• Y

Step 1
Use a compass to measure the length of $\overline{XY}$.

Step 2
Draw a horizontal line through point W. From point W, use the compass measure of $\overline{XY}$ to draw an arc intersecting the line drawn. Label this intersection J. $\overline{WJ}$ is congruent to $\overline{XY}$.

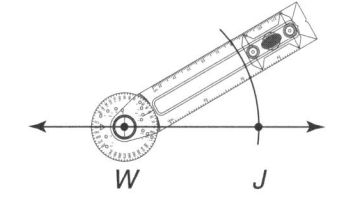

Example 2

Construct a perpendicular bisector of $\overline{AB}$.

A •————————• B

Step 1
Use a compass to measure more than half the length of $\overline{AB}$.

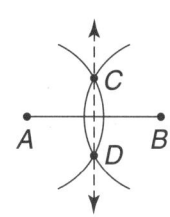

Step 2
From point A, draw an arc intersecting $\overline{AB}$. From point B, draw another arc intersecting $\overline{AB}$. Draw a line through the 2 points of intersection of the arcs. Label the points C and D. $\overleftrightarrow{CD}$ is the perpendicular bisector of $\overline{AB}$.

---

1. Construct a segment congruent to $\overline{XY}$.   X •————————————• Y

2. Construct the perpendicular bisector of $\overline{XY}$.

© Pearson Education, Inc.

111

Intervention Lesson **K56**

Name _____

Constructions (continued)

Example 3

Construct an angle congruent to ∠A.

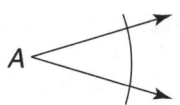

Step 1
Draw a ray with the endpoint S.

Step 2
From point A, use a compass to draw an arc intersecting both sides of ∠A. From point S, use the same compass measure to draw an arc intersecting the ray at point T.

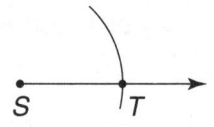

Step 3
Use a compass to measure the length of the arc intersecting both sides of ∠A. Use the same measure to draw an arc from T that intersects the first arc. Label the point R and draw the ray SR.

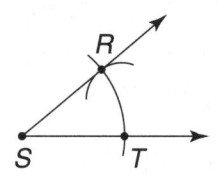

---

3. Construct an angle congruent to ∠J.

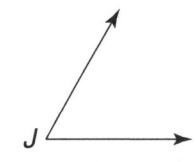

Test Prep Circle the correct letter for the answer.

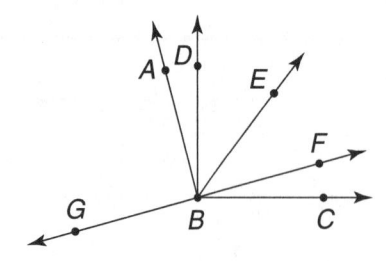

4. Which ray appears to be the bisector of angle ABC?
   A $\overrightarrow{BD}$ **B** $\overrightarrow{BE}$ **C** $\overrightarrow{BF}$ **D** $\overrightarrow{BG}$

5. Which angle appears to be congruent to angle ABG?
   A ∠ABE   **B** ∠EBC   **C** ∠DBC   **D** ∠FBC

Name _____

Intervention Lesson **K57**

Tessellations

A tessellation is a repeated geometric design. It covers a plane with no gaps or overlaps. Brick walls and tiled floors are examples of tessellations.

Example 1

Name the polygon used to form the tessellation below.

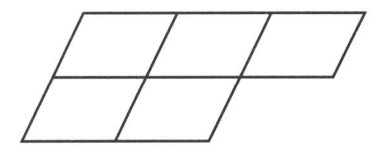

The tessellation is formed by a parallelogram.

Example 2

Use the pentagon shown below to demonstrate why a tessellation of regular pentagons is impossible.

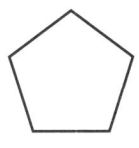

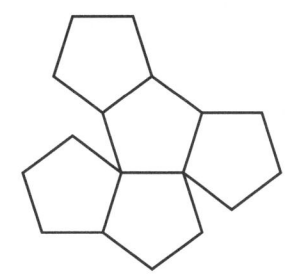

The tessellation is impossible because there are gaps between the figures.

Draw a tessellation made of each polygon.
(Hint: You may need to rotate or flip the shape.)

1. square   **2.** hexagon   **3.** right triangle

113

Name _____

Math Diagnosis and Intervention System

Intervention Lesson **K57**

Tessellations (continued)

Does each shape tessellate? If so, trace the figure and draw the tessellation.

4.

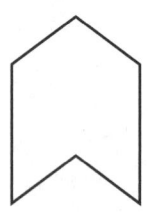

5.

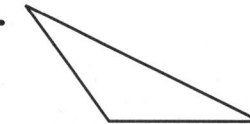

6.

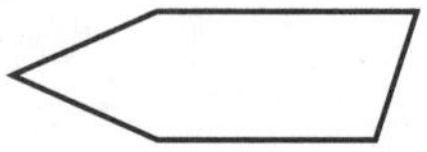

7.

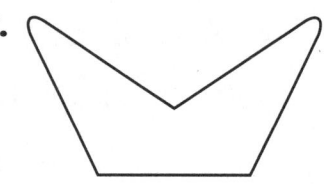

8.

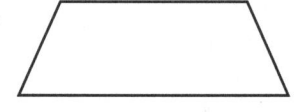

9.

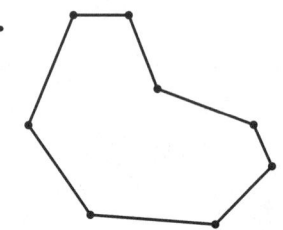

10. **Writing in Math** Kim says that an octagon (8-sided figure) does not tessellate. Is she right? Explain.

_____

_____

Test Prep Circle the correct letter for the answer.

11. Which of these figures does not tessellate?

   A hexagon   **B** parallelogram   **C** circle   **D** rectangle

114

Name _____

Math Diagnosis and Intervention System
Intervention Practice **K1**

Measuring Length to $\frac{1}{2}$ and $\frac{1}{4}$ Inch

Fill in the ○ with the correct answer.

Measure each to the nearest inch.

1. 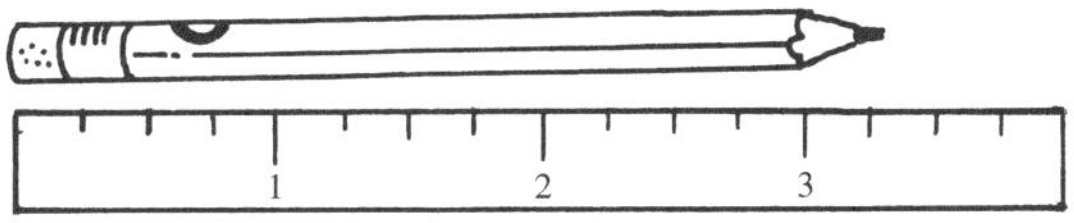
   ○ 1 inch   ○ 3 inches
   ○ 2 inches ○ 4 inches

2. 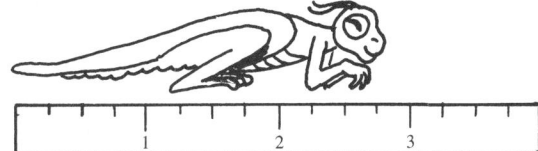
   ○ 1 inch   ○ 3 inches
   ○ 2 inches ○ 4 inches

Measure each to the nearest $\frac{1}{2}$ inch.

3. 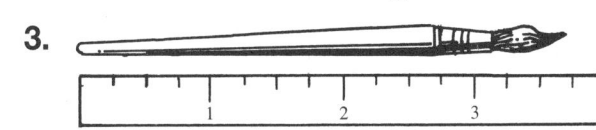
   ○ $2\frac{1}{2}$ inches ○ $3\frac{1}{2}$ inches
   ○ 3 inches   ○ 4 inches

4. 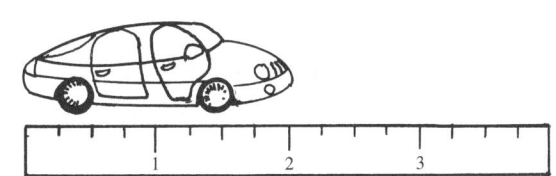
   ○ $1\frac{1}{2}$ inches ○ $2\frac{1}{2}$ inches
   ○ 2 inches   ○ 3 inches

Measure each to the nearest $\frac{1}{4}$ inch.

5. 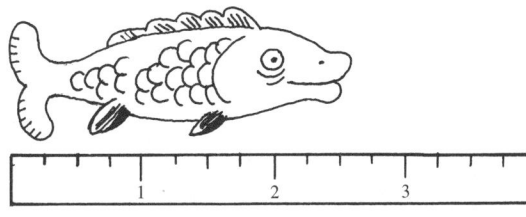
   ○ $2\frac{1}{4}$ inches ○ $2\frac{3}{4}$ inches
   ○ $2\frac{1}{2}$ inches ○ 3 inches

6. 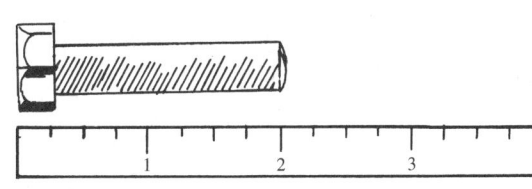
   ○ $1\frac{3}{4}$ inches ○ $2\frac{1}{4}$ inches
   ○ 2 inches   ○ $2\frac{1}{2}$ inches

© Pearson Education, Inc.

115

Name _____

Intervention Practice **K2**

Using Customary Units of Length

Circle the correct letter for the answer.

1. What is the length of the honey bee to the nearest half inch?

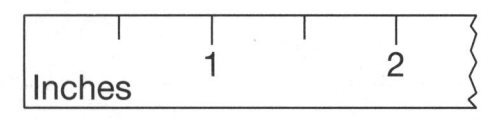

   A $\frac{1}{2}$ inch
   B 1 inch
   C $1\frac{1}{2}$ inches
   D $2\frac{1}{2}$ inches

2. What is the length of the nail to the nearest $\frac{1}{4}$ inch?

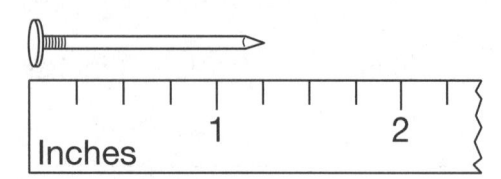

   A $\frac{1}{4}$ inch
   B $\frac{1}{2}$ inch
   C $1\frac{1}{4}$ inches
   D $1\frac{3}{4}$ inches

3. Which would be the best unit of measure to use to measure the length of a dollar bill?

   A Inch
   B Foot
   C Yard
   D Mile

4. How many inches are in 2 feet?

   A 18 inches
   B 20 inches
   C 24 inches
   D 72 inches

5. A vet measured the lengths of 3 dogs. Champ is 2 feet, Buster is 28 inches, and Spot is 21 inches. Which of the following statements is true?

   A Spot and Champ are the same length.
   B Champ is 36 inches long.
   C Spot is longer than Buster.
   D Buster is longer than Champ.

116

Name _____

Math Diagnosis and Intervention System
Intervention Practice **K3**

Measure to $\frac{1}{8}$ Inch

Circle the correct letter for the answer.

1. Which is the measurement to the nearest $\frac{1}{8}$ inch?

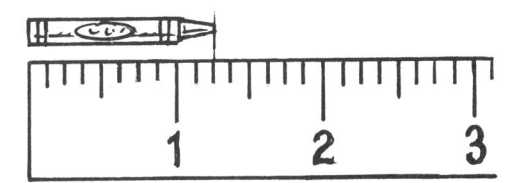

   A   1 inch   C $1\frac{1}{4}$ inches
   B $1\frac{1}{8}$ inches   D $1\frac{1}{2}$ inches

2. Which is the measurement to the nearest $\frac{1}{4}$ inch?

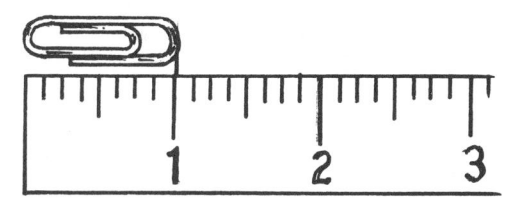

   A $\frac{1}{2}$ inch   C $\frac{3}{4}$ inch
   B   1 inch   D $1\frac{1}{4}$ inches

3. Which is the measurement to the nearest $\frac{1}{8}$ inch?

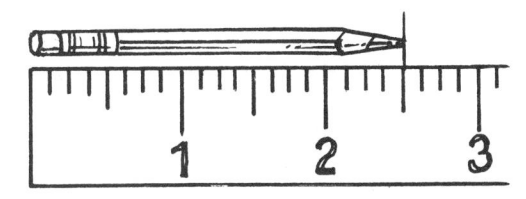

   A   2 inches   C $2\frac{1}{4}$ inches
   B $2\frac{1}{2}$ inches   D $2\frac{1}{8}$ inches

4. Which is the measurement to the nearest $\frac{1}{4}$ inch?

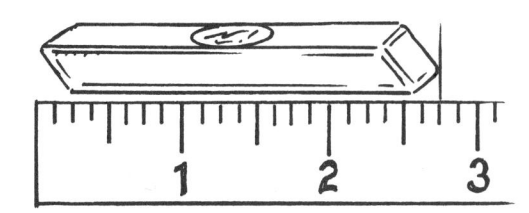

   A   3 inches   C $2\frac{3}{4}$ inches
   B $2\frac{3}{8}$ inches   D $2\frac{1}{2}$ inches

5. Which is the measurement to the nearest $\frac{1}{8}$ inch?

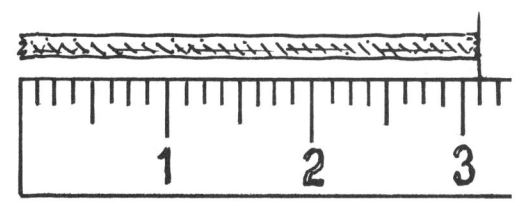

   A $3\frac{1}{4}$ inches   C $3\frac{1}{8}$ inches
   B $2\frac{3}{8}$ inches   D $2\frac{1}{8}$ inches

6. Which is the measurement to the nearest $\frac{1}{4}$ inch?

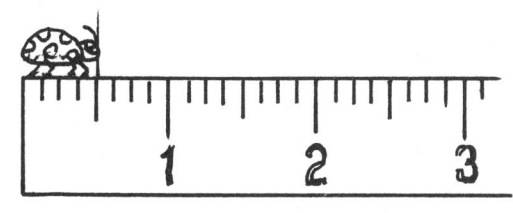

   A $\frac{1}{8}$ inch   C $\frac{1}{2}$ inch
   B $\frac{1}{4}$ inch   D   1 inch

117

Customary Units of Measurement

Circle the correct letter for the answer.

1. Complete.
   57 feet = ■ yards
   A 171
   B 114
   C 19
   D 18

2. Fred has 24 quarts of milk. How many 1-gallon containers can he fill?
   A 6
   B 12
   C 48
   D 96

3. Brittany bought 5 gallons of distilled water. How many quarts is that?
   A 40 quarts
   B 20 quarts
   C 10 quarts
   D 1.25 quarts

4. A commercial jet is at an altitude of 26,400 feet. How many miles is that?
   A 2 miles
   B 5 miles
   C 10 miles
   D 50 miles

5. Larry is buying ice cream for 36 people at a birthday party. If the serving size will be about $\frac{1}{2}$ cup, how many quarts of ice cream should he buy?
   A 5
   B 4
   C 3
   D 2

6. Use the diagram for Question 6.

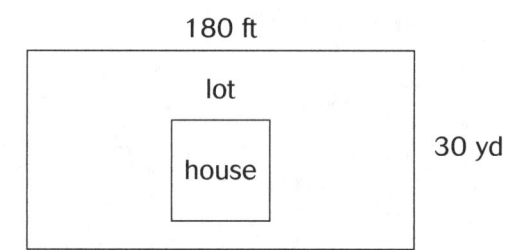

   180 ft / lot / house / 30 yd

   The lot is 30 yards wide. The house is half as wide as the lot. What is the width of the house in feet?
   A 60 feet
   B 45 feet
   C 15 feet
   D 5 feet

Name _____

Intervention Practice **K5**

Using Metric Units of Length

Circle the correct letter for the answer.

1. What is the length of the worm to the nearest centimeter?

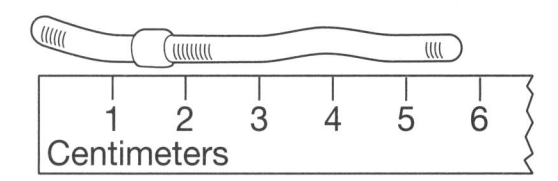

   A 3 centimeters
   B 4 centimeters
   C 5 centimeters
   D 6 centimeters

2. Which is the best estimate for the length of a child's wagon?

   A 1 centimeter
   B 1 meter
   C 1 kilometer
   D 10 meters

3. Which length is greatest?

   A 200 centimeters
   B 8 decimeters
   C 2,000 meters
   D 1 kilometer

4. Jeremy thinks 1 meter is greater than 125 centimeters. Julie thinks 125 centimeters is greater than 1 meter. Which statement is true?

   A They are both incorrect.
   B They are both correct.
   C Jeremy is correct.
   D Julie is correct.

5. Which is the best estimate for the distance walked in 2 hours?

   A 8 centimeters
   B 8 meters
   C 8 kilometers
   D 80 kilometers

6. Estimate the length of the bone.

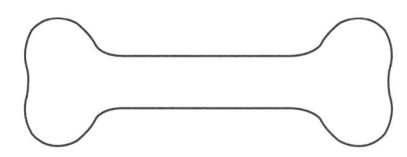

   A 2 centimeters
   B 5 centimeters
   C 2 decimeters
   D 5 decimeters

Name _____

Using Customary Units of Capacity

Circle the correct letter for the answer.

Use the pictures to answer Questions 1–3.

[MILK gallon] [Grape Juice 1 pint] [Spring Water 1 quart]

1. If you buy 2 containers of grape juice, how many cups of grape juice will you have?

    A   1 cup
    B   4 cups
    C   2 cups
    D   8 cups

2. If you buy 8 bottles of spring water, how many gallons will you have?

    A   1 gallon
    B   2 gallons
    C   4 gallons
    D   8 gallons

3. What is the best estimate for the container of milk?

    A   1 cup
    B   1 pint
    C   1 quart
    D   1 gallon

4. How many pints are in 1 gallon?

    A   2 pints
    B   4 pints
    C   8 pints
    D   16 pints

5. What is the best unit of capacity for the amount of water in a pond?

    A   Cups
    B   Pints
    C   Quarts
    D   Gallons

6. What is the best estimate for the amount of juice in a juice box?

    A   1 cup
    B   1 pint
    C   1 quart
    D   1 gallon

7. Cathy needs 4 cups of milk to make pudding. How many pints of milk does she need?

    A   1 pint
    B   2 pints
    C   3 pints
    D   4 pints

Name _____

Intervention Practice **K7**

Using Milliliters and Liters

Circle the correct letter for the answer.

1. Which is the best estimate for the amount of milk in a milk carton?
   - **A** 1 liter
   - **B** 1 milliliter
   - **C** 10 milliliters
   - **D** 10 liters

2. Greg has 2 liters of apple juice. He drinks 250 milliliters of the juice. How much juice is left?
   - **A** 248 milliliters
   - **B** 750 milliliters
   - **C** 1,250 milliliters
   - **D** 1,750 milliliters

3. Which measurement is the least?
   - **A** 3,000 milliliters
   - **B** 2 liters
   - **C** 2,500 milliliters
   - **D** 1,999 milliliters

4. Which is the best estimate for the amount of liquid in a tablespoon?
   - **A** 5 milliliters
   - **B** 500 milliliters
   - **C** 5 liters
   - **D** 50 liters

5. You have an iced tea container that holds 1 liter. You put 325 milliliters of iced tea in it. How much more iced tea will fit in the container?
   - **A** 525 milliliters
   - **B** 675 milliliters
   - **C** 855 milliliters
   - **D** 1,325 milliliters

6. Which measurement is greatest?
   - **A** 2 liters
   - **B** 2 milliliters
   - **C** 3 liters
   - **D** 2,990 milliliters

Name _____

Intervention Practice **K8**

Using Ounces and Pounds

Circle the correct letter for the answer.

1. A box of cereal weighs 13 ounces. A bag of potato chips weighs 1 pound. How much more does the bag of potato chips weigh than the box of cereal?

    A 1 ounce
    B 2 ounces
    C 3 ounces
    D 5 ounces

2. Helen bought 2 pounds of potatoes. How many ounces do the potatoes weigh?

    A 16 ounces
    B 32 ounces
    C 48 ounces
    D 24 ounces

3. Which is the best estimate for the weight of a volleyball?

    A 1 ounce
    B 9 ounces
    C 9 pounds
    D 90 pounds

4. Your math textbook weighs about 32 ounces. About how much would 2 textbooks weigh?

    A 2 pounds
    B 3 pounds
    C 4 pounds
    D 5 pounds

5. Which of the following items weighs about 1 pound?

    A A marshmallow
    B A jar of spaghetti sauce
    C A large sack of flour
    D A sack full of groceries

6. Which of these weights is the same as 3 pounds?

    A 16 ounces
    B 32 ounces
    C 36 ounces
    D 48 ounces

Name _____

Intervention Practice **K9**

Using Grams and Kilograms

Circle the correct letter for the answer.

1. Which item would you weigh using kilograms?

    A Dime
    B Pencil
    C Computer
    D Feather

2. Which is heaviest?

    A 1,256 grams
    B 2 kilograms
    C 987 grams
    D 3 kilograms

3. Jeremy has 3 boxes with the following weights: 854 grams, 623 grams, and 520 grams. *About* how heavy are the boxes in all?

    A 1 kilogram
    B 2 kilograms
    C 3 kilograms
    D 4 kilograms

4. Which is the best estimate for the mass of a telephone?

    A 1 kilogram
    B 1 gram
    C 100 kilograms
    D 100 grams

5. One cereal box is about 327 grams. How many more grams would it have to be to weigh 1 kilogram?

    A 664 grams
    B 673 grams
    C 783 grams
    D 1,327 grams

6. Which item weighs about 1 kilogram?

    A Bicycle
    B Ring
    C Book
    D Postcard

Metric Units of Measurement

Circle the correct letter for the answer.

1. 5 km = _____ m
   - A   500
   - B   5,000
   - C   50,000
   - D   5,000,000

2. 97 mm = _____ cm
   - A   9,700
   - B   970
   - C   9.7
   - D   0.97

3. The length of a football field is 109.09 m. How many centimeters is this?
   - A   10.909
   - B   1090.9
   - C   1.0909
   - D   10,909

4. The height of the Empire State Building is 381 m. How tall is it in kilometers?
   - A   0.381
   - B   3.81
   - C   38.1
   - D   3,810

5. The width of a key on a calculator is 0.5 cm. How many millimeters is this?
   - A   5
   - B   500
   - C   0.5
   - D   0.005

6. Which measurement is the largest?
   - A   1.2 m
   - B   1,100 mm
   - C   140 cm
   - D   0.1 dam

7. 7,500 m = _____ km
   - A   7.5
   - B   75
   - C   750
   - D   7,500

8. 27 cm = _____ mm
   - A   2.7
   - B   270
   - C   2,700
   - D   27,000

Name _____

Math Diagnosis and Intervention System
Intervention Practice **K11**

Time to the Quarter-Hour

Fill in the ○ for the correct answer.

1. What time is shown?

   ○ 7:45   ○ 7:15
   ○ 8:15   ○ 3:00

2. Look at the pattern. What time comes next?

   4:00   4:15   3:30   4:30
   ○   ○   ○   ○

3. What clock shows 8:45?

   ○   ○   ○   ○

125

Name _____

Math Diagnosis and Intervention System

Intervention Practice **K12**

Telling Time

Fill in the ○ for the correct answer.

1. What time is shown?

    ○ 10 minutes after 2   ○ 5 minutes after 2

    ○ 5 minutes before 2   ○ quarter to 2

2. What time is shown?

    ○ 20 minutes before 12   ○ quarter to 12

    ○ 20 minutes before 11   ○ 20 minutes after 12

3. What time is shown?

    ○ 10 minutes before 8   ○ quarter to 8

    ○ 10 minutes after 8   ○ quarter to 7

4. Which clock shows 10 minutes before 4?

    ○   ○   ○   ○

126

Telling Time

Circle the correct letter for the answer.

1. Which is the time shown on the clock?

   A quarter after two
   B quarter to two
   C quarter to three
   D half past three

2. Which is the time shown on the clock?

   A half past six
   B quarter to six
   C half past four
   D half past five

3. Which is the time shown on the clock?

   A quarter to five
   B quarter to four
   C quarter after four
   D half past four

4. Which is the same as half past two?

   A 2:15   C 2:30
   B 2:45   D 2:50

5. Which is the same as ten to seven?

   A 6:50   C 7:10
   B 9:37   D 10:07

6. Which is a good time to eat lunch?

   A 2:00 A.M.   C 9:00 A.M.
   B 12:30 P.M.   D 5:55 P.M.

127

Units of Time

Circle the correct letter for the answer.

Units of Time
1 minute = 60 seconds
1 hour = 60 minutes
1 day = 24 hours
1 week = 7 days
1 month = about 4 weeks
1 year = 52 weeks
1 year = 12 months
1 year = 365 days
1 leap year = 366 days
1 decade = 10 years
1 century = 100 years
1 millennium = 1,000 years

1. 36 weeks ■ 250 days
   A >   B <   C =

2. 5 decades ■ 55 years
   A >   B <   C =

3. 2 hours ■ 7,200 seconds
   A >   B <   C =

4. Bryan worked 42 hours this week. How many minutes did he work?
   A 2,400 min   C 2,800 min
   B 2,520 min   D 4,200 min

5. 4 years = ■ weeks
   A 208   C 52
   B 156   D 28

6. Summer vacation lasts 12 weeks. How many days is that?
   A 19   C 77
   B 60   D 84

7. 1 year 6 weeks = ■ days
   A 407   C 314
   B 371   D 58

8. Margaret Okayo ran the 2002 Boston Marathon in 2 hours, 20 minutes, 43 seconds. How many seconds is this?
   A 5,468 s   C 7,220 s
   B 2,602 s   D 8,443 s

Name _____

Math Diagnosis and Intervention System

Intervention Practice **K15**

Elapsed Time

Fill in the ○ for the correct answer.

1. Which clock shows 2 hours later than 12:00?

   12:00   2 hours later

   ○   ○   ○   ○

2. Which clock shows 1 hour and 30 minutes later than 10:00?

   10:00   1 hour and 30 minutes later

   ○   ○   ○   ○

3. Debbie started to play chess at 2:30. She finished at 4:00. How long did she play?

   ○ 1 hour   ○ 2 hours

   ○ 1 hour and   ○ 2 hours and
      30 minutes   30 minutes

129

Elapsed Time; Schedules

Circle the correct letter for the answer.

1. As her meeting started, Jessica looked at her watch, shown below. When the meeting stopped for lunch, it was 11:10. How much time had elapsed?

   A 1 h 40 min   C 1 h 20 min
   B 2 h 20 min   D 2 h 40 min

Use the table for Questions 2 and 3.

Bus Pick up Schedule	
Oak Street	7:53 A.M.
Elm Street	8:08 A.M.
Clark Street	8:12 A.M.
Lakewood Ave.	8:21 A.M.
School	8:39 A.M.

2. According to the schedule, if Henry lives on Elm Street, how long is his bus ride to school?

   A 8 minutes   C 27 minutes
   B 21 minutes   D 31 minutes

3. If Seneca gets on the bus at Oak Street, and Trisha gets on the bus 19 minutes later, where does Trisha get on?

   A Oak Street
   B Elm Street
   C Clark Street
   D Lakewood Ave

4. Subtract.   23 h 35 min
                − 15 h 17 min

   A 8 h 18 min   C 38 h 18 min
   B 38 h 52 min   D 8 h 52 min

5. Both clocks show times on Friday morning. How much time has elapsed?

   A 3 h 12 min   C 3 h 26 min
   B 2 h 26 min   D 3 h 14 min

6. Add.   30 h 28 min
          + 17 h 31 min

   A 12 h 57 min   C 48 h 9 min
   B 47 h 59 min   D 49 h 49 min

Name _____

Intervention Practice **K17**

Using a Calendar

December 2004						
Sunday	Monday	Tuesday	Wednesday	Thursday	Friday	Saturday
			1	2	3	4
5	6	7	8	9	10	11
12	13	14	15	16	17	18
19	20	21	22	23	24	25
26	27	28	29	30	31	

Circle the correct letter for the answer.

Use the calendar for December to answer Questions 1–4.

1. What date is the next day after December 6th?
   - **A** December 9th
   - **B** December 5th
   - **C** December 8th
   - **D** December 7th

2. What day of the week is December 13th?
   - **A** Sunday
   - **B** Monday
   - **C** Wednesday
   - **D** Thursday

3. What date is the second Wednesday in December?
   - **A** December 15th
   - **B** December 14th
   - **C** December 8th
   - **D** December 1st

4. What day of the week is the last day of December?
   - **A** Sunday
   - **B** Friday
   - **C** Thursday
   - **D** Saturday

5. How many days are in one week?
   - **A** 7 days
   - **B** 6 days
   - **C** 31 days
   - **D** 30 days

6. The Woodards are going on a family vacation for 1 week. If they start their trip on June 14th, on what date will they return?
   - **A** June 18th
   - **B** June 19th
   - **C** June 21st
   - **D** June 28th

7. Today is March 9th. Jaime has to go to the dentist in 5 days. On what date will he go to the dentist?
   - **A** March 12th
   - **B** March 13th
   - **C** March 15th
   - **D** March 14th

Time Zones

Circle the correct letter for the answer.

Use the clocks below for Questions 1–3.

7:00 A.M. Friday — Boston, Massachusetts
3:00 P.M. Friday — Moscow, Russia

1. What is the time in Moscow when it is 11:10 A.M. in Boston?
   - **A** 7:10 P.M.
   - **B** 3:00 P.M.
   - **C** 1:00 P.M.
   - **D** 6:00 A.M.

2. What is the time in Boston when it is 11:45 P.M. in Moscow?
   - **A** 8:15 P.M.
   - **B** 2:45 P.M.
   - **C** 3:45 P.M.
   - **D** 7:45 A.M.

3. Which statement is true?
   - **A** The time in Moscow is 8 hours behind the time in Boston.
   - **B** The time in Moscow is 8 hours ahead of the time in Boston.
   - **C** The time in Moscow is 10 hours ahead of the time in Boston.
   - **D** The time in Moscow is 10 hours behind the time in Boston.

Use the clocks below for Questions 4–6.

6:00 A.M. Monday — Mexico City, Mexico
1:00 P.M. Monday — Paris, France

4. What is the time in Paris when it is 10:25 A.M. in Mexico City?
   - **A** 5:25 A.M.
   - **B** 10:25 A.M.
   - **C** 1:00 P.M.
   - **D** 5:25 P.M.

5. What is the time in Mexico City when it is 3:50 P.M. in Paris?
   - **A** 8:50 A.M.
   - **B** 9:50 A.M.
   - **C** 8:50 P.M.
   - **D** 9:50 P.M.

6. Which statement is NOT true?
   - **A** When it is 5:00 P.M. in Mexico City it is 12:00 A.M. in Paris.
   - **B** When it is 5:00 P.M. in Paris it is 10:00 A.M. in Mexico City.
   - **C** When it is 5:00 A.M. in Mexico City it is 12:00 noon in Paris.
   - **D** When it is 5:00 A.M. in Paris it is 12:00 noon in Mexico City.

Converting Units

Circle the correct letter for the answer.

1. 300 cm =
   - A 3 km
   - B 3 m
   - C 3 mm
   - D 1 mm

2. Marcella's dog weighs 5 pounds 4 ounces. How many ounces is that?
   - A 54 ounces
   - B 80 ounces
   - C 84 ounces
   - D 540 ounces

3. Which statement is true?
   - A 1 cm = 1,000 m
   - B 3 L = 30 mL
   - C 20 g = 2 kg
   - D 4 cm = 40 mm

4. 4 c =
   - A 1 qt
   - B 2 qt
   - C 3 qt
   - D 4 qt

5. What is the mass in grams of a box with a mass of 4 kilograms?
   - A 4 grams
   - B 40 grams
   - C 400 grams
   - D 4,000 grams

6. Which statement is not true?
   - A 16 qt = 4 gal
   - B 3 yd 2 ft = 8 ft
   - C 2 c = 16 fl oz
   - D 2,100 lb = 2 T 100 lb

7. 4 L 200 mL =
   - A 4,200 mL
   - B 420 mL
   - C 42 mL
   - D 4 mL

8. How many feet long is a 3-mile track?
   - A 3,000 feet
   - B 5,280 feet
   - C 15,000 feet
   - D 15,840 feet

Temperature

Circle the correct letter for the answer.

1. Which word best describes the temperature on this thermometer?

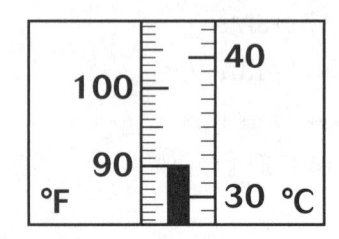

   A Hot
   B Cold
   C Warm
   D Cool

2. The temperature is 15°C. Which would you most likely wear?

   A Hat, gloves, and heavy coat
   B Sweater or sweatshirt
   C Bathing suit
   D Shorts and a tee shirt

3. At which temperature does water freeze?

   A 212°F
   B 20°C
   C 37°C
   D 32°F

4. What is the temperature in °C shown on this thermometer?

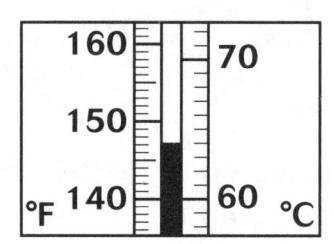

   A 147°C
   B 147°F
   C 64°C
   D 64°F

5. The temperature is 30°F in Denver, 77°F in Atlanta, 98°F in Mexico City, and 62°F in Trenton. In which city might you be able to build a snowman?

   A Denver
   B Atlanta
   C Mexico City
   D Trenton

6. At which temperature does water boil?

   A 212°F
   B 100°F
   C 32°C
   D 0°C

Name _____

Math Diagnosis and Intervention System
Intervention Practice **K21**

Temperature

Circle the correct letter for the answer.

1. Which temperature is shown?

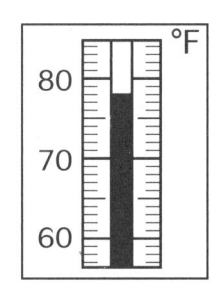

   A 83°F
   B 78°F
   C 75°F
   D 73°F

2. Which temperature is most appropriate for swimming at the beach?

   A ⁻3°C
   B 14°C
   C 34°C
   D 88°C

3. What is the difference between 29°F and 66°F?

   A 47°F
   B 43°F
   C 37°F
   D 33°F

4. Which temperature is equivalent to 32°C?

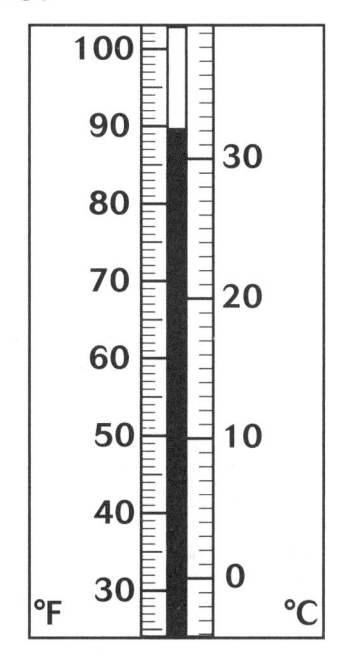

   A 0°F   C 32°F
   B 90°F   D 60°F

5. Which is the best estimate for the temperature of a cold glass of milk?

   A ⁻12°C   C 22°C
   B 2°C   D 44°C

6. The temperature at noon is 36°F. It was 9°F colder at 8:00 A.M. What was the temperature at 8:00 A.M.?

   A 45°F   C 33°F
   B 37°F   D 27°F

© Pearson Education, Inc.

135

Name _____

Intervention Practice **K22**

Math Diagnosis and Intervention System

Units of Measure and Precision

Circle the correct letter for the answer.

1. Which measurement is the most precise?

   A   2075 m
   B   2075.3 m
   C   2075.33 m
   D   2100 m

2. Which measurement is the most precise?

   A   3 in.
   B $4\frac{1}{4}$ in.
   C $3\frac{1}{8}$ in.
   D $3\frac{5}{16}$ in.

3. Which measurement is the most precise?

   A   pounds
   B   ounces
   C   kilograms
   D   grams

4. Which measurement of the object is the most precise?

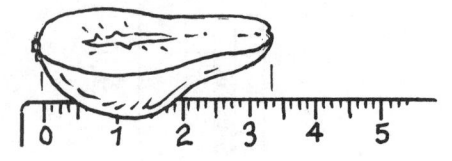

   A   4 cm
   B   4.5 cm
   C   47 mm
   D   50 mm

5. Which measurement of the object is the most precise?

   A $3\frac{5}{16}$ in.
   B $3\frac{1}{2}$ in.
   C   4 in.
   D $3\frac{1}{4}$ in.

6. Cari measured the distance between her desk and John's desk. These were the measurements. Which measurement is the most precise?

   A   18 inches
   B $18\frac{3}{16}$ inches
   C   46 cm
   D   463 mm

Converting Between Measurement Systems

Circle the correct letter for the answer.

1. 20 pounds is about ___?___ kilograms.
   - A 5
   - B 10
   - C 20
   - D 40

2. 8 inches is about ___?___ centimeters.
   - A 4
   - B 8
   - C 12
   - D 20

3. 0.5 meter is about ___?___ feet.
   - A $1\frac{1}{2}$
   - B 2
   - C $2\frac{1}{2}$
   - D 3

Use the list of materials below for Questions 4 and 5.

Throw Pillow
Materials Needed:
$\frac{1}{2}$ yd fabric, 45 in. wide
2 yd trim, 2 in. wide
8 oz fiberfill

4. *About* how much fabric, in meters, is needed to make 1 pillow?
   - A 2 meters
   - B $1\frac{1}{2}$ meters
   - C 1 meter
   - D $\frac{1}{2}$ meter

5. *About* how much fiberfill, in grams, is needed for 1 pillow?
   - A 50 grams
   - B 200 grams
   - C 1.5 grams
   - D 1,000 grams

Perimeter

Circle the correct letter for the answer.

1. Which is the perimeter of this rectangle?

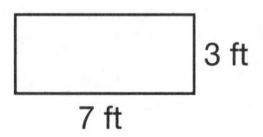

   3 ft
   7 ft

   A   10 feet
   B   17 feet
   C   20 feet
   D   21 feet

2. Which is the perimeter of this figure?

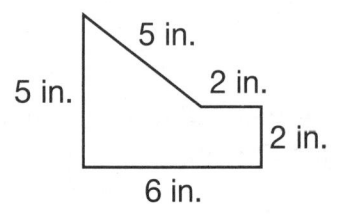

   5 in.
   5 in.
   2 in.
   2 in.
   6 in.

   A   11 inches
   B   13 inches
   C   20 inches
   D   30 inches

3. The sides of a square are 6 feet long. Which is its perimeter?

   A   36 feet
   B   24 feet
   C   12 feet
   D   6 feet

4. Harriet drew the sketch below of her flower garden. She wants to put a fence around the garden. How many feet of fencing does she need?

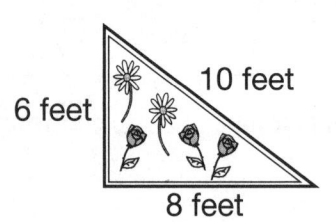

   6 feet   10 feet
             8 feet

   A   14 feet
   B   16 feet
   C   18 feet
   D   24 feet

5. Which is the perimeter of this figure?

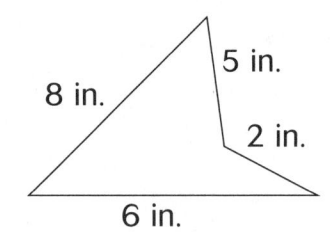

   8 in.   5 in.
            2 in.
   6 in.

   A   14 inches
   B   16 inches
   C   19 inches
   D   21 inches

Name _____

Intervention Practice K25

Area

Circle the correct letter for the answer.

1. Which is the area of the shaded figure?

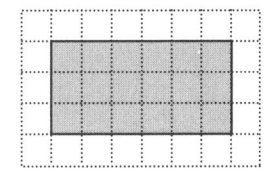

   A 9 square units
   B 12 square units
   C 18 square units
   D 24 square units

2. Which is the area of the shaded figure?

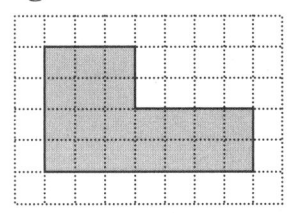

   A 28 square units
   B 20 square units
   C 18 square units
   D 15 square units

3. Which has the largest area?

   A A rectangle with 1 row of 5 squares.
   B A rectangle with 2 rows of 3 squares
   C A rectangle with 2 rows of 8 squares
   D A rectangle with 1 row of 2 squares

4. Which is the best estimate for the area of the shaded figure?

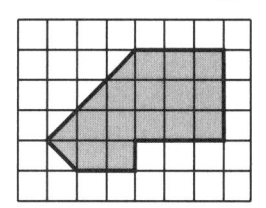

   A 13 square units
   B 14 square units
   C 16 square units
   D 18 square units

5. Your town is having a spring fair. There will be sections for crafts, games, face painting, and sales of homemade foods. Look at the plan of the fair below.

   Which section has the largest area?
   A Face painting
   B Games
   C Homemade food
   D Crafts

139

Name _____

Intervention Practice **K26**

Perimeter

Circle the correct letter for the answer.

1. Find the perimeter of this figure.

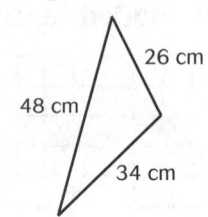

   26 cm
   48 cm
   34 cm

   A   60 cm
   B   82 cm
   C   98 cm
   D   108 cm

2. Sam has a rectangular garden. The garden is twice as long as it is wide. If the perimeter of the garden is 60 yards, what are the length and width of the garden?

   A   15 yards by 15 yards
   B   20 yards by 10 yards
   C   30 yards by 15 yards
   D   40 yards by 20 yards

3. A 12-inch-long rectangle has a perimeter of 32 inches. How wide is the rectangle?

   A   22 inches
   B   20 inches
   C   16 inches
   D   4 inches

4. Wendy is placing stones around a square garden. The garden measures 82 meters on each side. What is the perimeter of the garden?

   A   164 meters
   B   328 meters
   C   6,724 meters
   D   368 meters

5. Two sides of a triangle are each 8 cm long. The perimeter of the triangle is 24 cm. Find the length of the third side.

   A   8 cm
   B   16 cm
   C   10 cm
   D   12 cm

Circumference

Circle the correct letter for the answer.

1. Swimming Pool

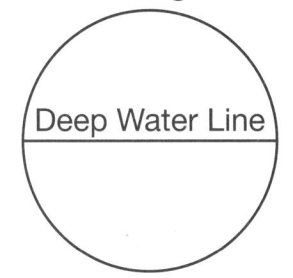

   The length of the deep water line is 28.5 meters. Find the circumference of the swimming pool.

   A 562.3 m
   B 89.49 m
   C 44.8 m
   D 57 m

2. What is the circumference of a circle with a diameter of 9 inches? Use 3.14 for π.

   A 56.52 in.
   B 14.13 in.
   C 81 in.
   D 28.26 in.

3.

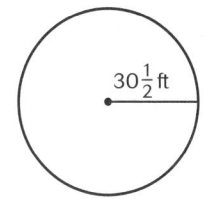

   Find the circumference of the circle. Use 3.14 for π.

   A 95.8 ft
   B 191.54 ft
   C 61 ft
   D 105.4 ft

4.

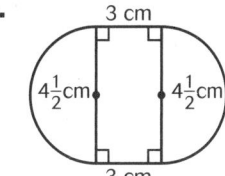

   Find the distance around the figure. Use 3.14 for π.

   A 20.13 cm
   B 15 cm
   C 29.1 cm
   D 47.1 cm

Area

Circle the correct letter for the answer.

1. Find the area of this figure.

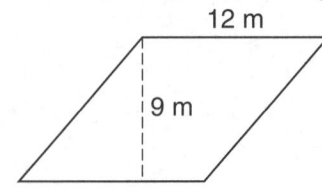

   12 m, 9 m

   A 21 m²
   B 42 m²
   C 108 m²
   D 216 m²

2. Find the area of this figure.

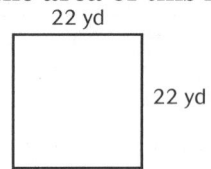

   22 yd, 22 yd

   A 44 yd²
   B 484 yd²
   C 88 yd²
   D 242 yd²

3. The area of a rectangle is 330 square inches. Its length is 15 inches. Find its width.

   A 150 inches
   B 160 inches
   C 22 inches
   D 24 inches

4. A parallelogram has height 4 meters and base 36 meters. Find its area.

   A 142 m²
   B 144 m²
   C 152 m²
   D 164 m²

5. Lidia's walk-in closet has an area of 18 square feet. Which could be the length and width of Lidia's closet?

   A $l = 6$ ft, $w = 12$ ft
   B $l = 9$ ft, $w = 9$ ft
   C $l = 5$ ft, $w = 4$ ft
   D $l = 3$ ft, $w = 6$ ft

6. A 16-foot-long rectangle has an area of 128 square feet. How wide is the rectangle?

   A 4 feet
   B 6 feet
   C 8 feet
   D 56 feet

Area

Circle the correct letter for the answer.

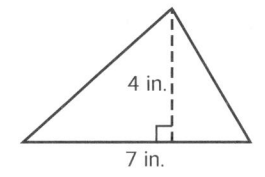

1. Find the area of the triangle.

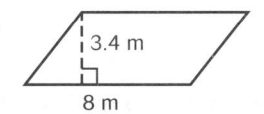

   A 56 in.²
   B 28 in.²
   C 14 in.²
   D 30 in.²

2. Find the area of a parallelogram.

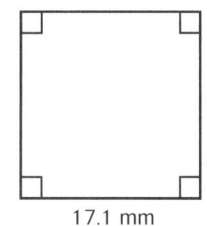

   A 13.6 m²
   B 54.4 m²
   C 27.2 m²
   D 24.1 m²

3. Find the area of the square.

   A 292.41 mm²
   B 34.2 mm²
   C 68.4 mm²
   D 312.51 mm²

4. A triangle has an area of 37.5 square feet and a height of 10 feet. What is its base?

   A 3.75 feet
   B 87.5 feet
   C 18.75 feet
   D 7.5 feet

5. Find the side of a square if its area is 169 cm².

   A 13 centimeters
   B 84.5 centimeters
   C 169 centimeters
   D 26 centimeters

Name _____

Math Diagnosis and Intervention System
Intervention Practice **K30**

Areas of Irregular Figures

Circle the correct letter for the answer.

1. Jack is putting down new carpet in the family room shown below. Which is the area of the family room?

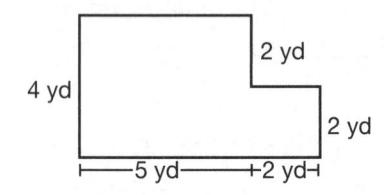

   A 15 yd²
   B 22 yd²
   C 24 yd²
   D 28 yd²

2. Laura is tiling the bathroom shown below with square tiles that are 1 square foot in area. How many tiles will she need?

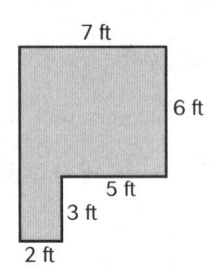

   A 41 tiles
   B 48 tiles
   C 63 tiles
   D 99 tiles

3. Which is the area of the figure given below?

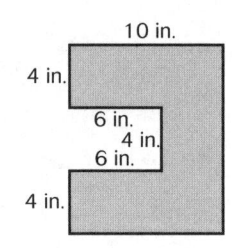

   A 96 in.²
   B 104 in.²
   C 112 in.²
   D 120 in.²

4. Celia is buying new carpet for the room shown below. If carpet costs $20 per square yard, how much will it cost her to carpet the room?

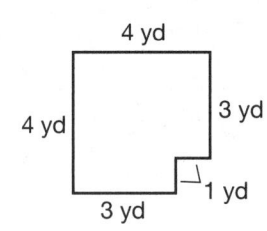

   A $200
   B $300
   C $460
   D $520

Rectangles with the Same Area

Circle the correct letter for the answer.

Use the figure below to answer Questions 1 and 2.

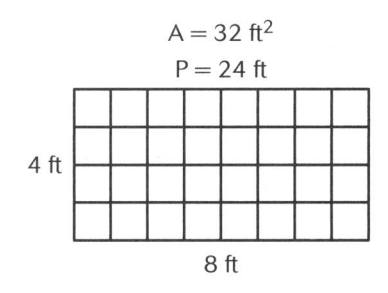

A = 32 ft²
P = 24 ft
4 ft
8 ft

1. Which are the dimensions of a rectangle with the same area as the given rectangle?

   A 16 ft × 2 ft
   B 6 ft × 4 ft
   C 12 ft × 2 ft
   D 16 ft × 16 ft

2. Which are the dimensions of a rectangle with the same perimeter as the given rectangle?

   A 6 ft × 4 ft
   B 12 ft × 12 ft
   C 9 ft × 3 ft
   D 8 ft × 3 ft

Use the rectangle below to answer Questions 3 and 4.

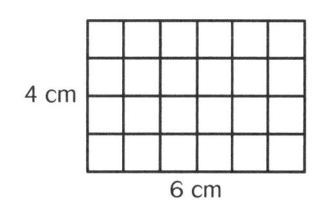

4 cm
6 cm

3. Which is the perimeter of the rectangle above?

   A 24 cm   **C** 12 cm
   B 20 cm   **D** 10 cm

4. Which of these rectangles has the same area as the rectangle above?

   A 3 cm, 4 cm
   B 2 cm, 6 cm
   C 4 cm, 5 cm
   D 3 cm, 8 cm

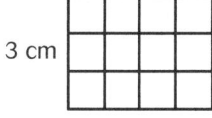

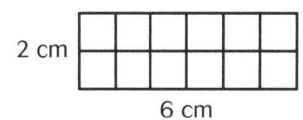

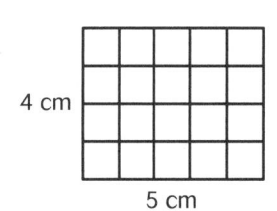

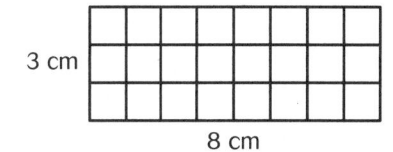

Name _____

Math Diagnosis and Intervention System
Intervention Practice **K32**

Area of a Circle

Circle the correct letter for the answer.

1.

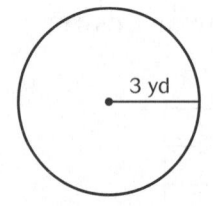

   (circle with radius 3 yd)

   Find the area of the circle. Round to the nearest whole number.

   A 19 yd²
   B 21 yd²
   C 28 yd²
   D 27 yd²

2.

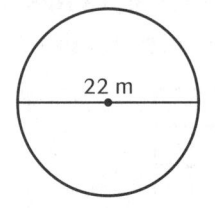

   (circle with diameter 22 m)

   Find the area of the circle. Round to the nearest tenth.

   A 380 m²
   B 69 m²
   C 1,520 m²
   D 35 m²

3.

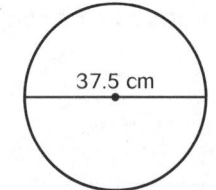

   (circle with diameter 37.5 cm)

   Find the area of the circle. Round to the nearest whole number.

   A 118 cm²
   B 4,416 cm²
   C 1,104 cm²
   D 59 cm²

4.

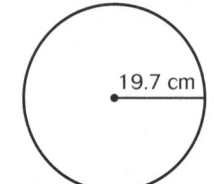

   (circle with radius 19.7 cm)

   Find the area of the circle. Round to the nearest whole number.

   A 62 cm²
   B 4,874 cm²
   C 124 cm²
   D 1,219 cm²

Surface Area

Circle the correct letter for the answer.

1. 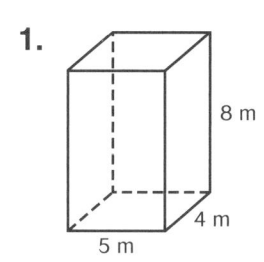 Find the surface area of the rectangular prism. (8 m × 5 m × 4 m)

   A 160 m²
   B 92 m²
   C 184 m²
   D 289 m²

2. Rosa wants to cover the cube-shaped box below with aluminum foil. She wants to use just enough foil to cover the box, without any waste. How many square inches of aluminum foil will she need?

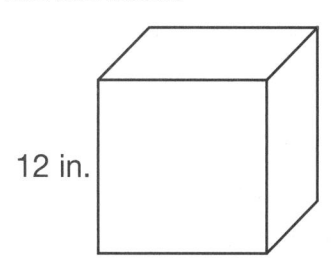

   (12 in. cube)

   A 144 in.²
   B 576 in.²
   C 864 in.²
   D 1,728 in.²

3. What is the surface area of a cereal box that measures 2 inches wide, 8 inches long, and 11 inches high?

   A 252 in.²
   B 176 in.²
   C 136 in.²
   D 126 in.²

4. 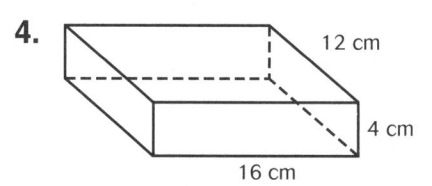 Find the surface area of the rectangular prism. (12 cm × 16 cm × 4 cm)

   A 768 cm²
   B 608 cm²
   C 32 cm²
   D 304 cm²

5. Find the surface area of a cube with 6 foot edges.

   A 216 ft²
   B 432 ft²
   C 108 ft²
   D 54 ft²

Name _____

Math Diagnosis and Intervention System
Intervention Practice **K34**

Comparing Volume and Surface Area

Circle the correct letter for the answer.

Use the figure for Questions 1 and 2.

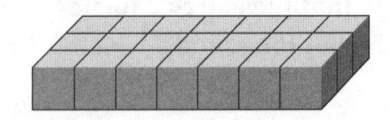

1. Which is the surface area?

   A   62 square units

   B   28 cubic units

   C   31 square units

   D   21 cubic units

2. Which is the volume?

   A   3 cubic units

   B   42 cubic units

   C   21 cubic units

   D   62 cubic units

Use the figure for Questions 3 and 4.

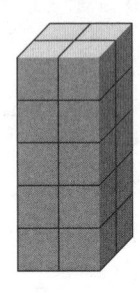

3. Which is the surface area?

   A   96 square units

   B   24 square units

   C   48 square units

   D   20 square units

4. Which is the volume?

   A   20 cubic units

   B   10 cubic units

   C   18 cubic units

   D   48 cubic units

Use the figure for Questions 5 and 6.

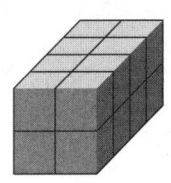

5. Which is the surface area?

   A   80 square units

   B   20 square units

   C   40 square units

   D   16 square units

6. Which is the volume?

   A   80 cubic units

   B   20 cubic units

   C   40 cubic units

   D   16 cubic units

Name _____

Intervention Practice **K35**

Volume

Circle the correct letter for the answer.

1. How many cubes were used to build this figure?

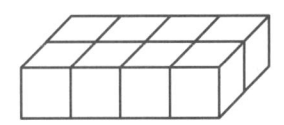

    A   4
    B   6
    C   8
    D   10

2. Which is the volume of the following figure?

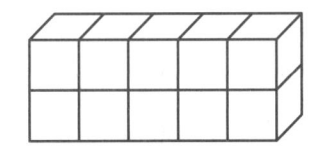

    A   5 cubic units
    B   10 cubic units
    C   20 cubic units
    D   30 cubic units

3. Which is the volume of the following figure?

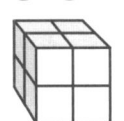

    A   4 cubic units
    B   6 cubic units
    C   8 cubic units
    D   10 cubic units

4. How many cubes were used to build this figure?

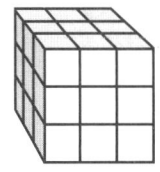

    A   36
    B   27
    C   18
    D   9

5. A box holds exactly 35 toy building blocks. Each block is in the shape of a cube. Which is the volume of the box?

    A   35 cubic units
    B   70 cubic units
    C   5 cubic units
    D   7 cubic units

6. Which has the greatest volume?

    A   4 cubes placed side-by-side
    B   A stack of 5 cubes
    C   4 cubes placed one on top of another
    D   2 rows of 3 cubes

149

Name _____

Intervention Practice **K36**

Volume

Circle the correct letter for the answer.

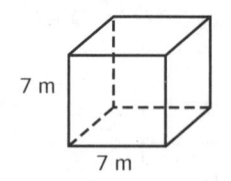

1. Find the volume of the cube.

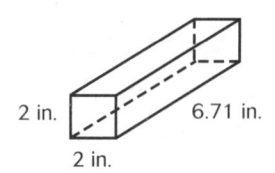

   7 m, 7 m

   A 343 m³
   B 51 m³
   C 21 m³
   D 172 m³

2. Find the volume of the rectangular prism.

   2 in., 6.71 in., 2 in.

   A 24.4 in.³
   B 48.4 in.³
   C 26.84 in.³
   D 53.68 in.³

3. Find the missing measurement.

   $l = 3\frac{1}{2}$ mm
   $w = 1\frac{1}{2}$ mm
   $h = \blacksquare$
   $V = 21$ mm³

   A 16 millimeters
   B 8 millimeters
   C 4 millimeters
   D 6 millimeters

4. Find the volume of a bathtub 3 feet wide, 5 feet long, and $2\frac{1}{2}$ feet deep.

   A $20\frac{1}{2}$ ft³
   B $37\frac{1}{2}$ ft³
   C $17\frac{1}{2}$ ft³
   D $27\frac{1}{2}$ ft³

Volume of Triangular Prisms and Cylinders

Circle the correct letter for the answer.

1.

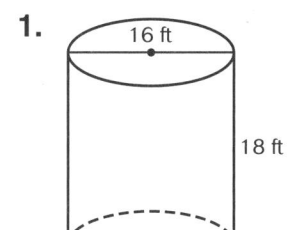

Find the volume of the cylinder.

A 4,608 ft³
B 3,617.28 ft³
C 1,152 ft³
D 45.8 ft³

2.

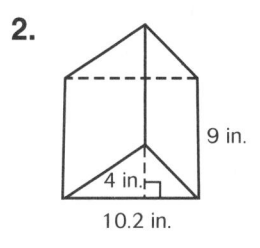

Find the volume of the triangular prism.

A 183.6 in.³
B 367.2 in.³
C 91.8 in.³
D 208.4 in.³

3.

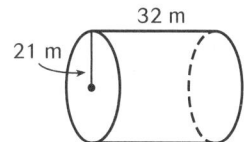

Find the volume of the cylinder.

A 672 m³
B 44,311.68 m³
C 11,083.5 m³
D 32,046.5 m³

4.

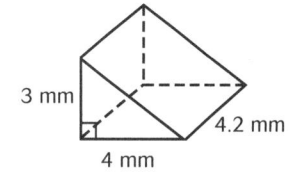

Find the volume of the triangular prism.

A 12.6 mm³
B 100.8 m³
C 25.2 mm³
D 50.4 mm³

Name _____

Math Diagnosis and Intervention System
Intervention Practice **K38**

Solid Figures

Circle the correct letter for the answer.

1. Name this solid figure.

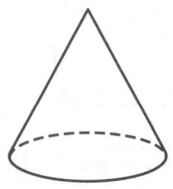

   A Sphere
   B Rectangular prism
   C Cone
   D Pyramid

2. Which object is shaped like a rectangular prism?

   A A pine log
   B A shoe box
   C A glass for milk
   D A soccer ball

3. Which solid figure is a pyramid?

   A 
   B 
   C 
   D

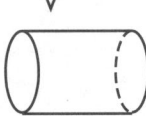

4. Name this solid figure.

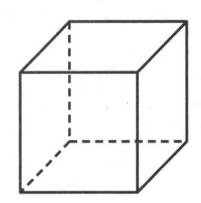

   A Cylinder
   B Cube
   C Pyramid
   D Sphere

5. Which solid figure does *not* have any edges?

   A Cube
   B Pyramid
   C Rectangular prism
   D Sphere

6. Which solid figure does *not* have any corners?

   A  Tomato Soup
   B (television)
   C  Raisins
   D (die)

152

Name _____

Math Diagnosis and Intervention System

Intervention Practice **K39**

Lines, Segments, Rays, and Angles

Circle the correct letter for the answer.

1. Name this angle.

   A Acute
   B Right
   C Obtuse
   D Straight

2. How many right angles are shown in the figure below?

   A 1 right angle
   B 2 right angles
   C 3 right angles
   D 4 right angles

3. Name this angle.

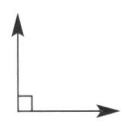

   A Right
   B Obtuse
   C Acute
   D Straight

4. How many right angles are shown in the figure below?

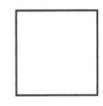

   A 0 right angles
   B 2 right angles
   C 4 right angles
   D 6 right angles

5. Which best describes the angle formed by the hands of the clock?

   A Acute
   B Right
   C Obtuse
   D Straight

6. Which best describes the angle formed by the letter V?

   V

   A Acute   C Obtuse
   B Right   D Straight

153

Plane Figures

Circle the correct letter for the answer.

1. Name the figure below.

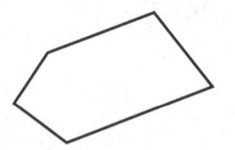

    A Square
    B Pentagon
    C Hexagon
    D Rectangle

2. How many sides does this figure have?

    A 0
    B 3
    C 4
    D 5

3. Which is a quadrilateral?
    A Square
    B Circle
    C Hexagon
    D Triangle

4. A painting has 6 sides and 6 corners. What shape is it?
    A Rectangle
    B Pentagon
    C Hexagon
    D Circle

5. Which statement is true?
    A A triangle has 4 sides.
    B A pentagon has 6 corners.
    C A rectangle has 5 sides.
    D A square has 4 corners.

6. Joanne got an answer of 9. Which problem did she do?
    A Find the total number of sides of a pentagon and a square.
    B Find the total number of sides of a triangle and a rectangle.
    C Find the total number of corners of a pentagon and a hexagon.
    D Find the total number of corners of two rectangles.

Name _____

Intervention Practice **K41**

Classifying Triangles Using Angles

Circle the correct letter for the answer.

1. Which figure is an acute triangle?

   A

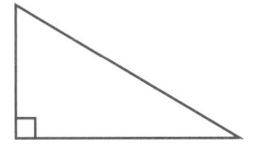

   B

   C

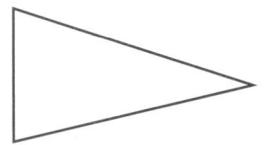

   D

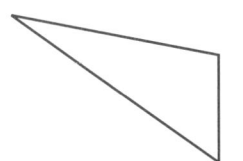

2. Which of the following best completes this sentence: An obtuse triangle has
   - A   One obtuse angle.
   - B   Two obtuse angles.
   - C   Three obtuse angles.
   - D   One right angle.

3. Which is the name of this figure?

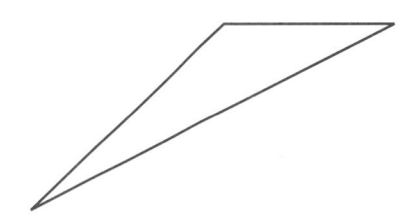

   - A   Acute triangle
   - B   Scalene triangle
   - C   Isosceles triangle
   - D   Right triangle

4. Which is the name of this figure?

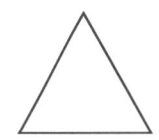

   - A   Acute angle
   - B   Scalene triangle
   - C   Obtuse triangle
   - D   Equilateral triangle

5. Which is the name of this figure?

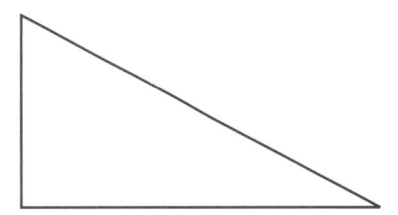

   - A   Equilateral triangle
   - B   Acute triangle
   - C   Obtuse triangle
   - D   Right triangle

Name _____

Intervention Practice **K42**

Quadrilaterals

Circle the correct letter for the answer.

Use Figures *A–D* for Questions 1 and 2.

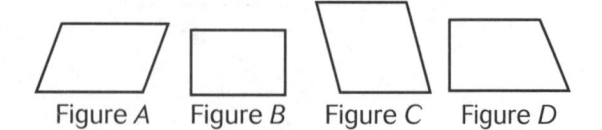

Figure A   Figure B   Figure C   Figure D

1. Which figure is a rhombus?

   A Figure *A*
   B Figure *B*
   C Figure *C*
   D Figure *D*

2. Which figure is a rectangle?

   A Figure *A*
   B Figure *B*
   C Figure *C*
   D Figure *D*

3. Which is the best name for this figure?

   A Parallelogram
   B Rhombus
   C Rectangle
   D Square

4. Which is the name of this figure?

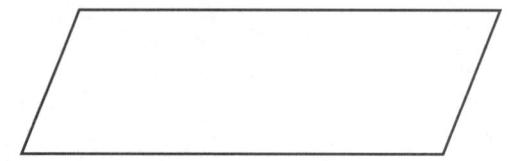

   A Parallelogram
   B Square
   C Rhombus
   D Rectangle

5. Which of these has 4 right angles and 4 equal sides?

   A Parallelogram
   B Rectangle
   C Square
   D Rhombus

6. Which of these has opposite sides which are parallel, and all sides the same length?

   A Parallelogram
   B Rectangle
   C Quadrilateral
   D Rhombus

156

Name _____

Intervention Practice **K43**

Slides, Flips, and Turns

Circle the correct letter for the answer.

1. Which describes how this figure was moved from A to B?

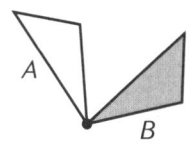

   A Slide
   B Flip
   C Turn
   D Flip then slide

2. Which of the following shows a reflection of the letter G across the dotted line?

   A 
   B 
   C 
   D

3. Which describes how this figure was moved from A to B?

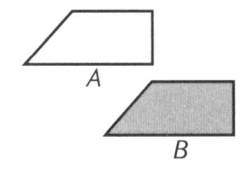

   A Slide
   B Flip
   C Turn
   D Flip then turn

4. Which of the following shows a turn?

   A 
   B 
   C 
   D

Name _____

Math Diagnosis and Intervention System
Intervention Practice **K44**

Line Symmetry

Circle the correct letter for the answer.

1. How many lines of symmetry does this figure have?

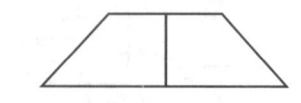

   A 0
   B 1
   C 2
   D 3

2. Which is NOT true about the following shapes?

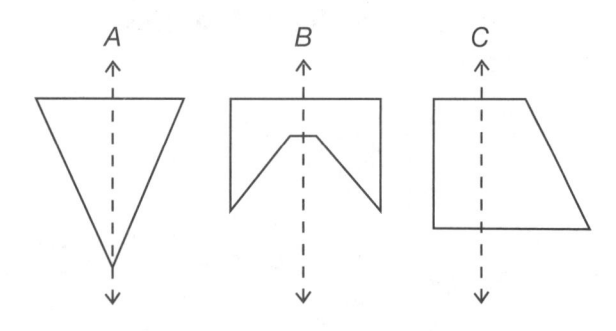

   A Shape B has only one line of symmetry.
   B Shape A and Shape B have lines of symmetry.
   C Shape C has a line of symmetry.
   D The two parts in Shape A match exactly.

3. Which flower has one line of symmetry?

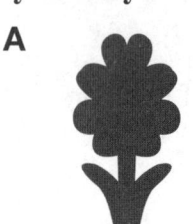

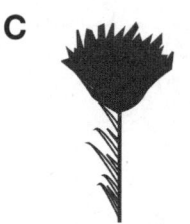

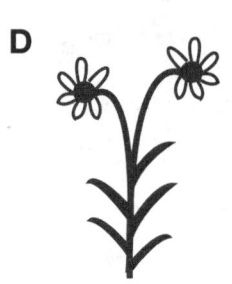

4. Heather is making a nature symmetry matching game. Which of these objects can she use?

   A Butterfly
   B Snowflake
   C Rock
   D Both A and B

5. Which letter has more than one line of symmetry?

   A The letter M
   B The letter T
   C The letter E
   D The letter O

158

Name _____

Math Diagnosis and Intervention System
Intervention Practice **K45**

Polygons

Circle the correct letter for the answer.

1. Which of the following is NOT a polygon?

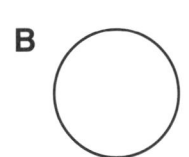

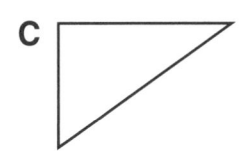

   A ☐ (square)

   B ○ (circle)

   C △ (triangle)

   D ▭ (rectangle)

2. I am the same shape as a stop sign. I am a polygon. I have 8 sides. What is my name?

   A Octagon
   B Pentagon
   C Quadrilateral
   D Triangle

3. Nikki is arranging her pencils to make a polygon. What is the fewest number of pencils she will need?

   A 1   C 3
   B 2   D 4

4. What is the name of this figure?

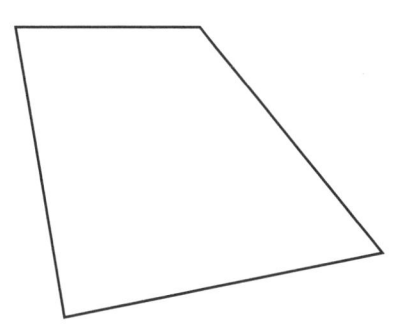

   A Octagon   C Quadrilateral
   B Pentagon   D Triangle

5. What is the name of this figure?

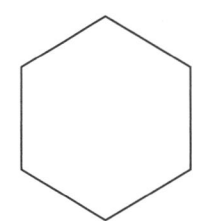

   A Rectangle   C Hexagon
   B Pentagon   D Octagon

6. I am the shape of a famous building in Arlington, Virginia. I am named for a polygon. I have 5 sides. What is my name?

   A Octagon
   B Pentagon
   C Quadrilateral
   D Triangle

159

Geometric Ideas

Circle the correct letter for the answer.

Use the figure for Questions 1 and 2.

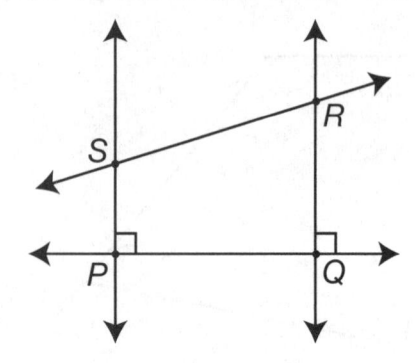

1. Name a line perpendicular to $\overleftrightarrow{RQ}$.
   A $\overleftrightarrow{SR}$
   B $\overleftrightarrow{SP}$
   C $\overrightarrow{PQ}$
   D $\overleftrightarrow{QR}$

2. Name a ray.
   A $\overrightarrow{PQ}$
   B $\overleftrightarrow{PQ}$
   C $\overrightarrow{PR}$
   D $\overleftrightarrow{SR}$

3. Which of these is a line segment shown in the figure? 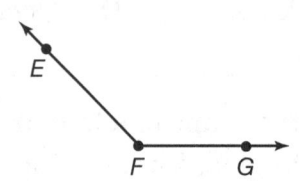
   A $\overleftrightarrow{FE}$
   B $\overrightarrow{FG}$
   C $\overline{EF}$
   D $\overline{GE}$

4. How would you name the figure? 
   A Ray VU
   B Ray UV
   C Line segment VU
   D Line VU

Use the figure for Questions 5 and 6.

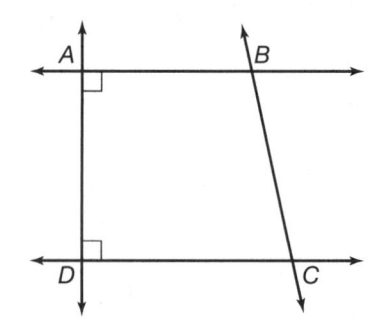

5. Which line is perpendicular to $\overleftrightarrow{AB}$?
   A $\overleftrightarrow{AB}$
   B $\overleftrightarrow{BC}$
   C $\overleftrightarrow{DB}$
   D $\overleftrightarrow{AD}$

6. Which line appears to be parallel to $\overleftrightarrow{AB}$?
   A $\overleftrightarrow{BC}$
   B $\overleftrightarrow{AC}$
   C $\overleftrightarrow{DB}$
   D $\overleftrightarrow{DC}$

Intervention Practice K47

Circles

Circle the correct letter for the answer.

Use this circle for Questions 1–3.

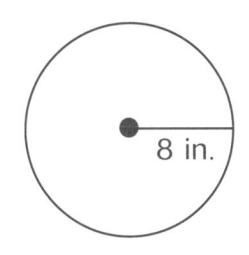

(circle with radius labeled 8 in.)

1. Which is the length of the radius?

   A 4 inches
   B 6 inches
   C 8 inches
   D 16 inches

2. Which is the length of the diameter?

   A 4 inches
   B 6 inches
   C 8 inches
   D 16 inches

3. Which is a true statement about the circumference of the circle?

   A It is about twice the radius.
   B It is about three times the radius.
   C It is about three times the diameter.
   D It is the radius plus the diameter.

4. A Ferris wheel has a radius of 15 feet. About what is its circumference?

   A About 90 feet
   B About 60 feet
   C About 30 feet
   D About 15 feet

5. The diameter of a pizza is 15 inches. What is its circumference?

   A About 30 inches
   B About 45 inches
   C About 50 inches
   D About 60 inches

6. Which is the radius of the circle?

   (circle with diameter labeled 16 in.)

   A 4 inches
   B 8 inches
   C 16 inches
   D 32 inches

Math Diagnosis and Intervention System

Intervention Practice K48

Name _____

Congruent and Similar Figures

Circle the correct letter for the answer.

1. Look at the pairs of figures below. Which figures within a pair appear to be similar?

   A 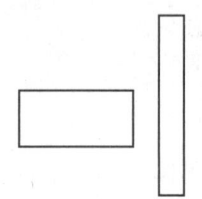
   B 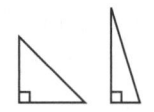
   C 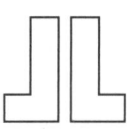
   D

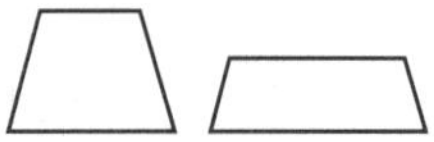

2. Look at the pairs of figures below. Which figures within a pair appear NOT to be congruent?

   A  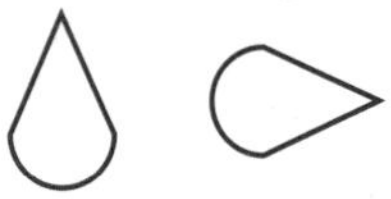
   B 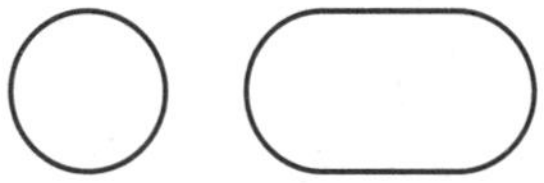
   C 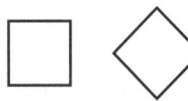
   D

3. Which is a true statement about these two circles?

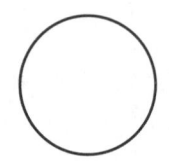

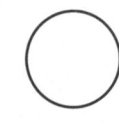

   A They have the same diameter.
   B They have the same radius.
   C They are congruent.
   D They are similar.

4. Which could show 4 congruent squares?

   A Folding a square piece of paper in half
   B Folding a square piece of paper in half twice
   C Folding a triangle in half
   D Folding a rectangle in half

5. Which figure could be similar to a 2-ft by 2-ft square?

   A 12-in. by 12-in. square
   B 1-ft by 3-ft rectangle
   C 10-in. by 24-in. rectangle
   D 12-in. by 24-in. rectangle

Intervention Practice K49

Measuring and Classifying Angles

Circle the correct letter for the answer.

1. Which is the measure of this angle?

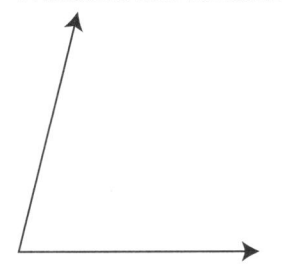

   A 105°   C 75°
   B 95°   D 45°

2. Classify this angle.

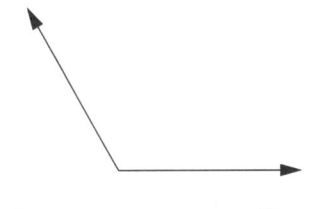

   A Obtuse   C Right
   B Acute   D Straight

3. Which angle has R as its vertex?

   A ∠QRS
   B ∠RQP
   C ∠PSR
   D ∠SPQ

Use the figure for Questions 4–6.

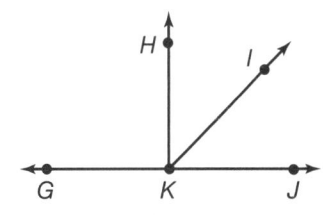

4. Which angle is an obtuse angle?

   A ∠GKH
   B ∠GKI
   C ∠JKI
   D ∠JKH

5. Which angle is a straight angle?

   A ∠GKI
   B ∠GKJ
   C ∠IKG
   D ∠IKJ

6. What kind of angle is ∠HKI?

   A Acute
   B Obtuse
   C Right
   D Straight

163

Name _____

Math Diagnosis and Intervention System
Intervention Practice **K50**

Triangles

Circle the correct letter for the answer.

1. Name this triangle.

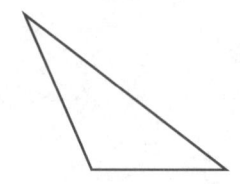

   A   Acute triangle
   B   Right triangle
   C   Obtuse triangle
   D   Isosceles triangle

2. Name this triangle.

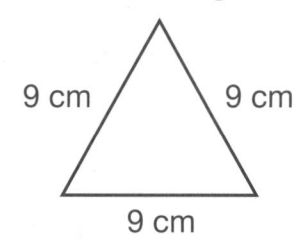

   9 cm   9 cm
   9 cm

   A   Equilateral triangle
   B   Isosceles triangle
   C   Scalene triangle
   D   Triangular prism

3. A triangle has sides of 3 centimeters, 4 centimeters, and 5 centimeters. Which kind of triangle is it?

   A   Equilateral triangle
   B   Isosceles triangle
   C   Scalene triangle
   D   Triangular prism

4. Which triangle is isosceles but not equilateral?

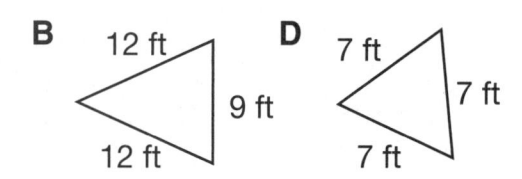

   A   6 ft, 2 ft, 5 ft
   C   10 ft, 6 ft, 8 ft
   B   12 ft, 9 ft, 12 ft
   D   7 ft, 7 ft, 7 ft

5. A garden has sides of 12 feet, 10 feet, and 12 feet. Which kind of triangle is formed by the sides of the garden?

   A   Equilateral triangle
   B   Isosceles triangle
   C   Right triangle
   D   Scalene triangle

6. Name this triangle.

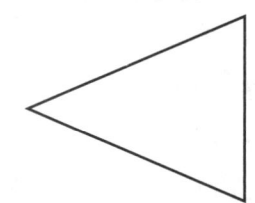

   A   Acute triangle
   B   Right triangle
   C   Obtuse triangle
   D   Equilateral triangle

© Pearson Education, Inc.

Name _____

Math Diagnosis and Intervention System

Intervention Practice **K51**

Quadrilaterals

Circle the correct letter for the answer.

1. Which is the name of this quadrilateral?

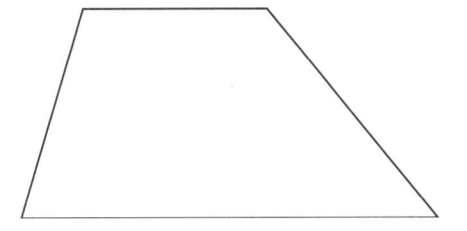

   A   Trapezoid
   B   Rectangle
   C   Rhombus
   D   Parallelogram

2. Which is the name for this shaded quadrilateral?

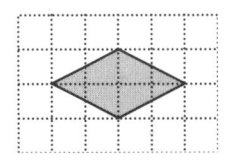

   A   Rhombus
   B   Square
   C   Rectangle
   D   Trapezoid

3. I am a quadrilateral. I have only one pair of parallel sides. What is my name?

   A   Rectangle
   B   Parallelogram
   C   Trapezoid
   D   Rhombus

4. Which of these shaded quadrilaterals is a parallelogram?

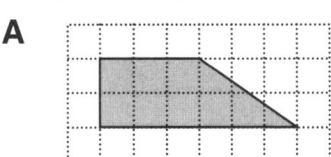

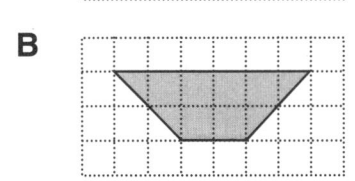

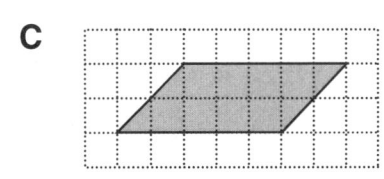

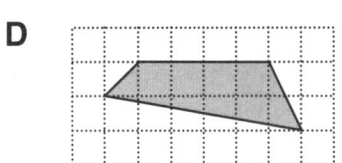

   A

   B

   C

   D

5. I am a quadrilateral. I have all sides with the same length. I have 4 right angles. What am I?

   A   Parallelogram
   B   Rhombus
   C   Rectangle
   D   Square

165

Name _____

Intervention Practice **K52**

Transformations

Circle the correct letter for the answer.

Use Figures *A–F* for Questions 1 and 2.

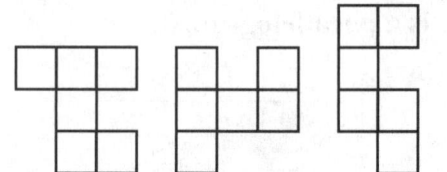

Figure *A*   Figure *B*   Figure *C*

Figure *D*   Figure *E*   Figure *F*

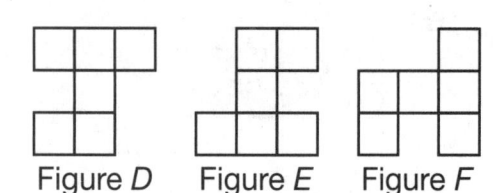

1. Which of these is a turn of Figure *A*?

   A Figure *C*   **C** Figure *E*
   B Figure *D*   **D** Figure *F*

2. Which of these is a flip of Figure *A*?

   A Figure *B*   **C** Figure *E*
   B Figure *C*   **D** Figure *F*

3. Identify the transformation.

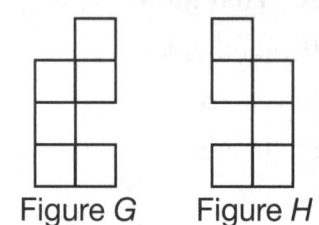

   Figure *G*   Figure *H*

   A $\frac{1}{4}$ turn
   B flip
   C slide
   D $\frac{3}{4}$ turn

4. Identify the transformation.

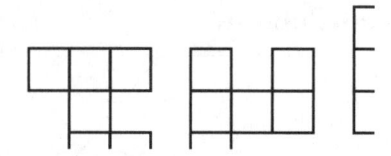

   A $\frac{1}{2}$ turn   **C** slide
   B flip   **D** $\frac{1}{4}$ turn

5. Identify the transformation.

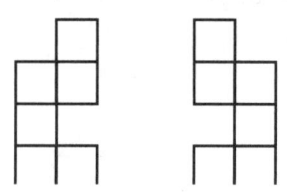

   A $\frac{1}{2}$ turn   **C** slide
   B flip   **D** $\frac{1}{4}$ turn

6. Identify the transformation.

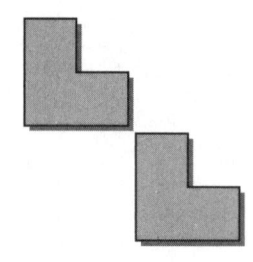

   A $\frac{1}{2}$ turn
   B flip
   C slide
   D $\frac{1}{4}$ turn

Solid Figures

Circle the correct letter for the answer.

1. Which of these statements is true for a triangular prism?

   A It has 2 parallel triangular bases.
   B It has 2 parallel rectangular bases.
   C All faces are triangles.
   D It has 1 triangular base and 3 triangular sides.

Use the figure for Questions 2 and 3.

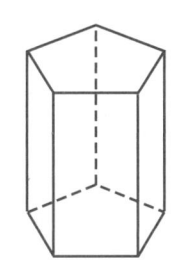

2. Which is the name of this figure?

   A Rectangular pentagon
   B Rectangular prism
   C Pentagonal prism
   D Pentagonal pyramid

3. Which of these statements is true for this figure?

   A The 2 parallel bases are rectangles.
   B Five of the faces are pentagons.
   C Three of the faces are rectangles.
   D Five of the faces are rectangles.

4. Which solid can be made from this net?

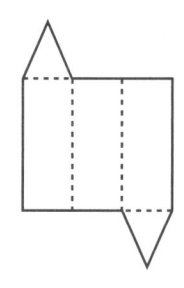

   A Rectangular prism
   B Rectangular pyramid
   C Triangular prism
   D Triangular pyramid

5. Which figure is a pentagonal prism?

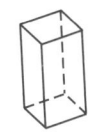

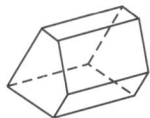

   Figure 1   Figure 2   Figure 3   Figure 4

   A Figure 2
   B Figure 3
   C Figure 4
   D Figure 1

6. Which shape is the base of a pyramid?

   A Parallelogram
   B Rectangle
   C Triangle
   D It depends on the type of pyramid.

167

Views of Solid Figures

Circle the correct letter for the answer.

1. Which solid will the net form?

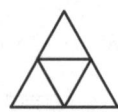

   A cube
   B rectangular prism
   C square pyramid
   D triangular pyramid

2. Which is the top view of the figure?

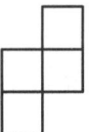

   A
   B 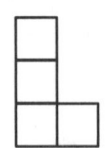
   C
   D

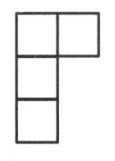

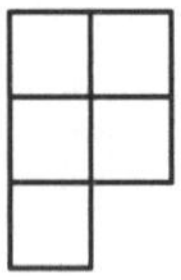

3. Which solid will the net form?

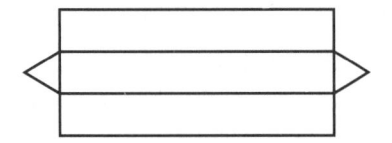

   A triangular pyramid
   B rectangular prism
   C triangular prism
   D square pyramid

4. Which is a side view of the figure?

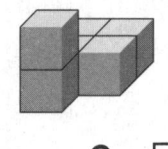

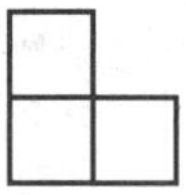

   A
   B 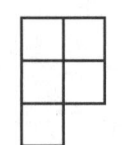
   C
   D

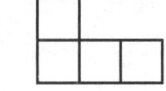

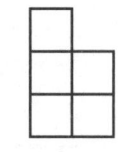

5. Which solid will the net form?

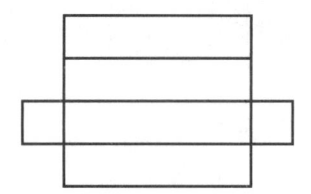

   A square pyramid
   B rectangular prism
   C cone
   D cube

6. Which solid will the net form?

   A cylinder
   B cone
   C square pyramid
   D sphere

168

Angle Pairs

Circle the correct letter for the answer.

1. What is the measure of the angle complementary to a 65° angle?
   - A 25°
   - B 35°
   - C 115°
   - D 205°

2. What is the measure of an angle supplementary to a 15° angle?
   - A 175°
   - B 75°
   - C 165°
   - D 85°

3. What is the measure of an angle complementary to a 20° angle?
   - A 160°
   - B 80°
   - C 30°
   - D 70°

4. What is the measure of an angle supplementary to a 44° angle?
   - A 136°
   - B 126°
   - C 46°
   - D 56°

Use this figure for Questions 5 and 6.

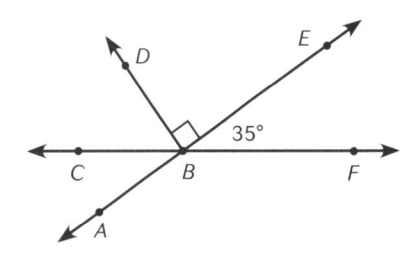

5. What is the measure of ∠CBA?
   - A 55°
   - B 35°
   - C 145°
   - D 65°

6. What is the measure of ∠ABD?
   - A 70°
   - B 145°
   - C 90°
   - D 55°

169

Name _____

Intervention Practice **K56**

Constructions

Circle the correct letter for the answer.

1. The drawing below shows how to

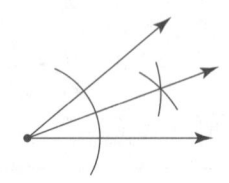

   A   construct a perpendicular bisector
   B   copy a segment
   C   construct congruent angles
   D   construct an angle bisector

2. Choose the step you would complete first to construct a segment congruent to segment $\overline{AB}$.

   A   Draw a ray.
   B   Measure the segment with a ruler.
   C   Draw points E and F.
   D   Open the compass the length of $\overline{AB}$.

3. $\overrightarrow{MR}$ bisects $\angle LMN$. If $m\angle LMN = 76°$, find $m\angle LMR$.

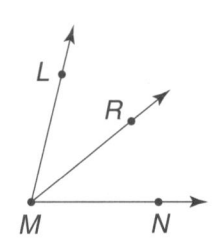

   A   152°   C   38°
   B   100°   D   24°

4. $\overline{AB}$ is the perpendicular bisector of $\overline{CD}$. If the length of $\overline{BD}$ is 15 inches, what is the length of $\overline{CD}$?

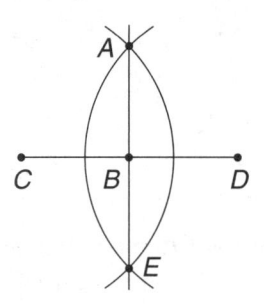

   A   7.5 inches   C   20 inches
   B   10 inches   D   30 inches

5. The drawing below shows how to

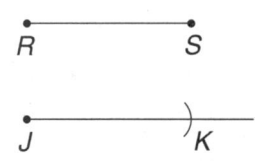

   A   construct a perpendicular bisector
   B   copy a segment
   C   construct congruent angles
   D   construct an angle bisector

6. Which statement is true?

   A   Congruent segments have different lengths.
   B   A perpendicular bisector divides a line equally.
   C   Congruent angles have different measures.
   D   A line segment has 1 endpoint.

170

Name _____

Intervention Practice **K57**

Tessellations

Circle the correct letter for the answer.

1. Which figure will *not* tessellate?

   A   square

   B   parallelogram

   C   hexagon

   D   octagon

2. How could you change the figure shown so that it will tessellate?

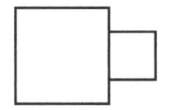

   A   Rotate the figure a $\frac{1}{4}$ turn.

   B   Add another small square to one side.

   C   Remove the small square.

   D   Rotate the figure a half turn.

3. Which statement is *not* true?

   A   A tessellation is a geometric design that has no gaps or overlaps.

   B   Brick walls are an example of a tessellation.

   C   A hexagon tessellates.

   D   Different figures that fill a plane create a tessellation.

4. Which of the figures will tessellate?

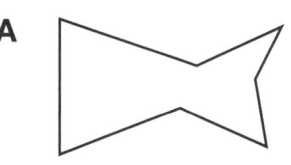

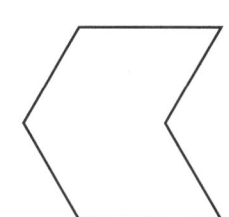

5. How could you change the figure shown so that it will tessellate?

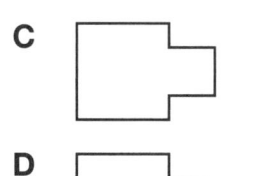

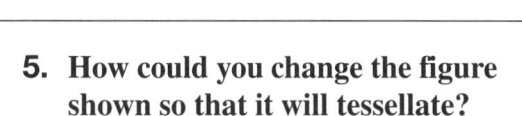

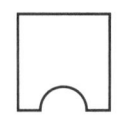

   A   Add a semicircle to the top of the figure.

   B   Rotate the figure half a turn.

   C   Add a triangle to the left side.

   D   Flip the figure.